Manage
Your Time
—— or ——
Time Will
Manage You

Manage Your Time

or

Time Will Manage You

STRATEGIES THAT WORK FROM AN
EDUCATOR WHO'S BEEN THERE

PJ CAPOSEY

Alexandria, Virginia USA

1703 N. Beauregard St. • Alexandria, VA 22311-1714 USA
Phone: 800-933-2723 or 703-578-9600 • Fax: 703-575-5400
Website: www.ascd.org • E-mail: member@ascd.org
Author guidelines: www.ascd.org/write

Deborah S. Delisle, *Executive Director,* Stefani Roth, *Publisher;* Genny Ostertag, *Director, Content Acquisitions;* Susan Hills, *Acquisitions Editor;* Julie Houtz, *Director, Book Editing & Production;* Jamie Greene, *Associate Editor;* Judi Connelly, *Associate Art Director;* Thomas Lytle, *Senior Graphic Designer;* Cynthia Stock, *Typesetter;* Mike Kalyan, *Director, Production Services;* Trinay Blake, *E-Publishing Specialist*

All web links in this book are correct as of the publication date below but may have become inactive or otherwise modified since that time. If you notice a deactivated or changed link, please e-mail books@ascd.org with the words "Link Update" in the subject line. In your message, please specify the web link, the book title, and the page number on which the link appears.

PAPERBACK ISBN: 978-1-4166-2665-7   ASCD product #119005   n8/18
PDF E-BOOK ISBN: 978-1-4166-2667-1; see Books in Print for other formats.
Quantity discounts: 10–49, 10%; 50+, 15%; 1,000+, special discounts (e-mail programteam@ascd.org or call 800-933-2723, ext. 5773, or 703-575-5773). For desk copies, go to www.ascd.org/deskcopy.

Library of Congress Cataloging-in-Publication Data

Names: Caposey, PJ, author.
Title: Manage your time or time will manage you : strategies that work from an educator who's been there / PJ Caposey.
Description: Alexandria : ASCD, [2018] | Includes bibliographical references and index.
Identifiers: LCCN 2018024307 (print) | LCCN 2018035480 (ebook) | ISBN 9781416626671 (PDF) | ISBN 9781416626657 (pbk.)
Subjects: LCSH: School administrators—Time management. | Educators—Time management.
Classification: LCC LB2831.658 (ebook) | LCC LB2831.658 .C36 2018 (print) | DDC 658.4/093—dc23
LC record available at https://lccn.loc.gov/2018024307

26 25 24 23 22 21 20 19 18   1 2 3 4 5 6 7 8 9 10 11 12

Manage Your Time

—— or ——

Time Will Manage You

Introduction

If you search Amazon for *time management*, you'll get over 40,000 results. If you do a Google search for *time management tips*, it provides 56 million responses in less than one second. If you search *time management* on Google Scholar, the search produces 4.8 million results. This begs the question, why in the world would anyone choose to produce more literature on a topic that is apparently so well covered already? My answer is simple. I think most people are examining time management from the wrong angle.

Like all of us, I am a sum of my experiences. As a novice school leader, I was working with one of my staff members, Danny, on some (perceived) time management issues. Danny was a hard worker, had an enormous amount of potential, and would consistently talk about how he truly wanted to be great at his job. Despite these conversations and qualities, Danny's work performance was defined by missing deadlines and dropping the ball on significant projects, along with a constant appearance of being overwhelmed and run down. While Danny was experiencing these struggles, there were several other team members with the same perceived level of capacity who were handling the challenges of the day quite well—and some were excited to continue to take on new and increasingly challenging tasks.

I began to have coaching conversations with Danny that became more pointed and frequent, hoping and believing that he could find the answer within himself and continue to move forward as a leader in our building. One month went by, two months went by, and the only thing that changed was the calendar. I soon began to look for some outside help with which to provide Danny. I read a handful of books and picked one for us to work through together that was full of practical tips and techniques. We completed a joint book study and within days I saw him start to implement some of the techniques we covered. I was excited and proud of the growth that was taking place. Then—as could have been predicted—after a few weeks of increased output, Danny returned to his typical behaviors.

Again, I was befuddled but not defeated. I did some more research and found a highly regarded seminar on time management sponsored by a top university. Despite the tight budget, I thought the potential within Danny was worth the price and sent him hundreds of miles away to a multiple-day seminar to reinforce and teach new time management techniques. Danny came back and informed me that it was time well spent. He said it reinforced many of the concepts taught in our book study, and he gained a few new tools for his teaching toolbox so he could start moving forward. Meanwhile, his colleagues were continuing to take on more responsibility and broadening the depth of their work while Danny was still trying to get out of his own way in order to move forward.

Weeks after returning from the conference, we arrived back at the previous status quo. Danny had missed another deadline and dropped the ball on a few key communication items, which damaged his reputation with both fellow staff members and the larger community. My mood was shaken and my confidence nearly lost in an individual I once thought had more potential than anyone else on my team. To be honest, my self-esteem was also a bit rattled. Why was I not able to help him?

I went home that night and was unable to shake off the bad day at work. My wife and I began to discuss the situation, and I said, "I have no idea what he could be doing with his time all day to get so far behind and let these major things fall through the cracks." My wife provided some simple yet profound advice: "Why don't you check?" I was confused. "Check what?" She explained that if I couldn't figure out where the problem was, then I should shadow him for a few days to find out.

That was it! I couldn't believe I hadn't thought of that before. Danny's time management issues were not presenting themselves as something I could understand (and I should have worked to understand the situation better before attempting to provide solutions), so I decided to follow Danny for two days to finally get clarity on what exactly was holding him back. It was awkward at first, but after the first few hours, we settled into a rhythm. The good news was that everything I hoped was not true was, in fact, not true. There were no seemingly intentional slights of duty. Danny was busy, professional, and continually engaged in what seemed like productive work.

I entered into this shadowing opportunity with the knowledge of what large projects Danny was supposed to be working on. That was a huge benefit, since I could see that he wasn't spending time on these major tasks and initiatives. Danny spent his day doing things like checking the hallways, wandering through rooms, checking in and following up with various kids, and building relationships with staff. Toward the end of the second day, Danny sat down to return some emails. As I sat behind him, I saw several emails (some I had sent) pinned to the top of his inbox (a technique we read about it in our book study). He looked right past those and returned several other emails before moving on with his day. That's when it hit me!

Danny didn't have trouble with time management. In fact, he managed his time perfectly to fit his strengths and goals. Danny had a major problem, I discovered, with work avoidance. It wasn't that Danny couldn't fit everything into the same amount of time his colleagues could; he simply chose not to do so. Instead, he filled his days with work-appropriate tasks but not goal-oriented tasks. I had misdiagnosed the issue and provided the wrong treatment. There was simply nothing I could have done in terms of tips, tricks, and techniques surrounding time management to have made Danny more efficient. My work with Danny wasn't helping him attack major projects and ensure his time usage met the goals set for him and the organization.

The major takeaway—and the one that led to writing this book—is that time management is not simple. It is a complex and extremely personal subject matter that can only be addressed through deep self-reflection or through caring and thoughtful coaching. This book, then, attempts to provide the platform and content to inspire deep introspection and provide tools for leaders and coaches to use as they work with others and continue to grow individually.

I believe strongly in tips, tricks, techniques, and seminars to help people become more efficient with their time, and I provide many of those techniques throughout this book. However, I operate from the paradigm that everybody manages their own time perfectly to get the results they want to achieve. As individuals and leaders, our challenge is more complex than many have tried to make it. If people aren't spending their time in a way that helps them accomplish their personal goals (or the goals set for them), then time management is only a symptom, not the disease.

This book attempts to identify and provide advice, support, and techniques for the common diseases that produce the symptom of time management difficulties. To better understand the symptom/disease analogy, consider the following scenario. What would happen if every time someone had a fever, he or she was given an aspirin and only an aspirin? The fever might immediately subside, it might eventually subside, it might manifest into different symptoms, or something critical or catastrophic could occur.

What is the point? The point is that every time someone has a fever, there is generally a reason for that fever to exist. An aspirin immediately treats a symptom—not the cause. In only a very few cases does treating the symptom alone solve the problem. Most of the time, it only serves to intensify the problem by masking the root cause. Take this analogy into the classroom, and it's possible for this to happen for so long that it starts to take great educators down a potentially career-altering path.

This book is divided into eight chapters. Each chapter details one of eight potential root causes of time management issues. Within each chapter, some self-diagnosis tips are provided as well as self-coaching and overall leadership strategies to employ when working with someone who is demonstrating these characteristics. A self-assessment is provided in Figure 0.1 for people to work toward self-diagnosis of their time management issues.

As you will see throughout the book, we all exhibit a little bit of all of these. There are times when I am checklist dependent, other times I seem perpetually distracted, and still other times where I find myself operating in a manner I enjoy, but that is not very productive. The intent of this book is to help each of us better understand ourselves and the behaviors that stop us from being more productive leaders. Because improving your productivity at work has the added benefit of decreasing your stress levels at home and in other endeavors, the advice in this book will help you not only work better but also *live* better.

This book is designed to be a partnership with the reader. It is perfectly acceptable to read the chapters out of order based on personal interest or current status. Enjoy!

Figure 0.1
Self-Assessment

- Place a 2 in the shaded area if you exhibit the behavior to a great extent.
- Place a 1 in the shaded area if you exhibit the behavior to a lesser extent.
- Leave the entire line blank if the behavior does not describe you.
- Total the columns upon conclusion.

Behavior	1	2	3	4	5	6	7	8
I will put down whatever I am working on no matter what to help a colleague in need.		�						
I have a checklist for every day and sometimes different checklists for different parts of the day.				▓				
I love every day at work and enjoy my typical daily responsibilities, but I never seem to get to my "real" work.							▓	
I spend time each day looking for a misplaced item.					▓			
I have an email in my inbox that I have looked at more than five times and have not yet completed the task.	▓							
Completing large tasks or tasks that involve considerable thought causes me stress.	▓							
I do not use an electronic calendar.						▓		
I check Facebook on my phone more than 20 times a day.			▓					
I have great time management skills for the work I like to do, but other areas suffer.							▓	
When I get organized at work, something seems to go wrong at home.								▓
I find myself losing 10–15 minutes a day checking social media, clicking on ads, or exploring apps when I did not intend to.			▓					

Behavior	1	2	3	4	5	6	7	8
I get a sense of joy each time I cross something off of my checklist or to-do list.				X				
I feel like I am the one who always gets delegated to, but I do not say anything in my defense.		X						
I can get in shape, but if I do, my effort at work suffers due to lack of time.								X
I wish I was able to say NO more often at work.		X						
If my cell phone beeps, it is painful to not instantly check the message or notification.			X					
I cannot see the majority of my desk.					X			
I choose getting work done over getting exercise and therefore am unhappy with how I look and feel.								X
I have over 100 emails in my inbox. (Note: two shaded areas to mark.)	X				X			
I know my job would be easier if I learned more about software and technology, but I am afraid to do so.						X		
I print all important documents and file them by hand.						X		
I do other people's work during the work day and my own work at night or on the weekends.		X						
I love small talk in the office or with colleagues.							X	
I am better at making checklists than completing the work on the checklists.				X				
I see other people using tech tools to make their life simpler, but I do not ask about them or take the time to learn how I could use them.						X		

continued

Figure 0.1
Self-Assessment (*continued*)

Behavior	1	2	3	4	5	6	7	8
I can't remember the last time that work, home, fitness, and spirituality were all working in concert with one another.								▓
Sometimes I feel like it takes me more time to make the checklist than to actually do the work.				▓				
I wear being disorganized as a badge of honor because I read somewhere that being disorganized is a sign of intelligence.					▓			
I sometimes find myself walking around in a circle between multiple tasks, often never finishing any of the tasks I am working on.			▓					
In a group email asking someone to complete a task, I NEVER reply first, hoping that someone else tackles the task.	▓							
I maintain great relationships with people at work, despite often being late or missing deadlines.							▓	
Totals								

Rank your scores to help determine what the root cause of your time management challenges might be, and pay particular attention to the chapters that focus on that cause:

- **Column 1:** Work Avoidant
- **Column 2:** People Pleaser
- **Column 3:** Prisoner of the Moment
- **Column 4:** Checklist Dependent
- **Column 5:** Disorganized
- **Column 6:** Technology Avoidant
- **Column 7:** Self-Server
- **Column 8:** Perpetually Imbalanced

1

Work Avoidant

Being work avoidant does not make you lazy. This is extremely important for everyone to understand. Being work avoidant simply means moving forward while ignoring key pieces of work that either do not interest you or are intimidating for some reason.

This book won't fix someone who is simply unwilling to do the incredibly complex work that educators must engage in daily to improve student outcomes. Rather, it is designed to help people better understand their own behaviors and create strategies that will allow them to better manage their time and, ultimately, lead to more productivity as leaders. It also provides practical solutions for people who are doing this great work—but doing it with a dramatic amount of stress. This is for the passionate educators and leaders who find themselves working an inordinate number of hours or are tired of having to approach their supervisor for extension after extension on key deadlines.

When I was growing up, my father would retreat to his home office approximately once a month with a pile of mail and a checkbook. Everyone in the house would take notice. There would be a series of phone calls, my mother would be called in a handful of times, and about three hours later my father would emerge. This end result usually went one of two ways. Either my father would rejoin us in a great mood, or he would emerge grumpy and we would be notified that the next few weeks were going to be "tight" (my father's code for "we're broke").

As I grew older and would rush to the mailbox as soon as the mailperson came in hopes of finding a magazine for me, I started to recognize what pieces of mail were bills that went into the pile that was set aside for my father's retreat. I remember thinking to myself when I was around 15 years old that it made no sense to keep those bills in a pile for weeks until an arbitrary day to pay them all came around. I vividly recall thinking how stressful that must have been in the weeks leading up to that day. Whenever we spent any money as a family, it must have been painful to think if that expense was going to make the next month's retreat painful or blissful for my father.

Fast-forward 10 years. I am 25 years old and doing my own bills on the floor of a house I could barely afford. I had fallen into the same cycle. Collect the bills all month and then ruin one Sunday morning as I figured out how broke I was. I can assure you that as a second-year teacher, it was often true that I was broke—*very* broke. I was trapped in my father's cycle not because it was what had been modeled for me but because I was afraid to open the envelopes when they were delivered. I was terrified of what the bills would show me. Instead of accepting the data of the bills immediately and then determining the next course of action, I waited until the last possible moment to open everything at once. In essence, I chose to feel a large amount of pain all at once instead of feeling a little bit of pain consistently. This is a very human tendency. We do it all the time!

For instance, if you have a wedding (or other event) you want to look great for in six months, you could try and lose four pounds per month—which is sizeable but eminently doable. Instead, most people do nothing for five months and then kill themselves the last four weeks trying to get the results they want. A lot of pain in a short amount of time is chosen over a little pain over a longer amount of time.

Housecleaning is another area where we all like to procrastinate. We all want to live in a nice, orderly living environment. We could spend 15 minutes a day before work, after work, or before bed straightening and potentially spot-cleaning one room. Alternatively, we could do nothing on those days and spend three hours every Sunday morning cleaning the house when we could be out for a walk, enjoying time with our family or reading a book. We choose to spend more time in a more intense way all at once instead of doing a little bit of work every day.

What does all of this mean and what does it have to with education? If each of the scenarios presented above—and the education-specific scenarios described throughout this chapter—make you react by saying, "Oh, my gosh, that's me!" then you may in fact be work avoidant and need to take steps to increase your productivity and decrease your personal stress. This is an important realization. Having "time management" issues is often perceived, and in some cases internalized, as lazy behavior. It is important to realize that such issues are incredibly draining and stressful to the person exhibiting the problematic behavior(s).

Signs You Are Work Avoidant

Almost everyone at work has some type of recurring deadline. For some, it may be turning in lesson plans every other Tuesday. For others, it may be turning in expense reports once a month. For still others, it may be loading lesson artifacts to the school website at the end of each school week. Whatever the recurring deadline looks like for you, odds are good that you have one. Although it is 100 percent possible to be work avoidant without a recurring deadline, such events provide a clear manner to discuss work avoidance.

As a superintendent of schools, I firmly believe in the value of proactive and clear communication. As a result, I mandate that each of my principals and department leaders sends out a weekly preview every Friday, detailing upcoming events to the building, extending thanks for extra effort, providing a few links to suggested reading, and including whatever else they believe people will find of value. I also do something similar with my bosses, the members of the board of education. Not only do I think this is a valuable exercise on behalf of those whom we serve, I also believe it helps focus us as leaders on what is truly important and keeps us always looking forward.

When I first made the weekly preview a performance expectation, many of my leaders had a look of dismay on their faces. Within a few months, many came to see its benefit and recognize that it came without a great deal of additional stress. I said *many*, however—not all. One leader continued to struggle to get the preview done before the end of business on Fridays. Sometimes it would come out on Saturday, sometimes on Sunday, and sometimes the weekly preview would come out Monday afternoon. Clearly, something was not working.

When I called him in to discuss the situation, I expected to hear that the weekly preview was not something he valued or cared about. I was wrong. Instead, it was something he cared deeply about but was causing him a great deal of stress. I asked how often he thought about the preview, and he replied that he thought about it every day. He sent himself email reminders, set aside time in his calendar, and even created a folder to collect potential topics until he was ready to create the document.

Because of this, I finally realized that work avoidance often has little to do with a perceived level of importance or laziness. It has much more to do with and is often the manifestation of one of four key levers triggering the behavior: skill deficits, grit, confidence, and the ability to self-monitor and self-correct negative behaviors. And the more of these triggering behaviors you have in a given situation, the more likely it is that the manifested behavior is one of work avoidance. Finally, keep in mind that what creates work avoidance within us is also what creates work avoidance among our students.

Skill Deficits

It is difficult to convince someone to complete a great deal of work in an area in which they do not feel skilled or accomplished. As a result, complex work is often avoided instead of practiced. This is a phenomenon that exists both within and outside education; however, there are additional pressures within education. As a building leader, there is a certain level of expected expertise. Likewise, as a teacher, there is a certain level of competency expected when it comes to curriculum, instruction, and content mastery. These expectations compound the stress normally felt with any level of skill deficit.

In my experience, areas in which a skill deficiency often leads to work avoidance include the following:

- Curriculum
- Instruction
- Best Practice
- Special Education
- Technology

These are areas where there are often not correct answers. It is easy to implement something that is black and white—that only has correct and incorrect answers or ways to approach the problem. By contrast, gray areas cause people to slow down, carefully consider their decisions, and often grind to a halt when they are not confident in their own judgment and abilities.

Grit

Grit is a concept that has been popularized within education during the last several years and is often discussed in conjunction with Carol Dweck's work regarding growth mindset. Dweck (2006) stated, "Mindset change is not about picking up a few pointers here and there. It's about seeing things in a new way. When people . . . change to a growth mindset, they change from a judge-and-be-judged framework to a learn-and-help-learn framework. Their commitment is to growth, and growth takes plenty of time, effort, and mutual support" (p. 254). Grit is simply the ability to fail forward and keep going. This is a skill being discussed and taught to children in many schools, but it should also be a focus for the adults in the building.

Grit dovetails with work avoidance since those who struggle to persist after a failure generally avoid completing that work again. This rings especially true for me and home repair work around the house. I recently attempted to mount a new television on the wall. I did everything the right way—just as I was taught. I went to drill a hole in a stud and instead went directly through the drywall, completely missing the stud. Instead of persisting, I quit until a friend came over later in the day to help. It turns out that I missed the stud by less than a quarter of an inch. If I had persisted, remeasured, and tried again, I would have successfully completed this task. Instead, I avoided the work. I found an easier way out. Paraphrasing Todd Whitaker (2012), I found a path of less resistance and pushed the work (and my stress) on to someone else. Instead of having grit, I shifted the monkey.

Confidence

Confidence does not always reflect ability. It often does, but occasionally it does not. For instance, anyone who plays sports has, at one time, had a teammate who had incredible confidence but little else to contribute. Likewise, it is possible to have tremendous ability but lack the confidence necessary to demonstrate your gifts. It should come as no surprise, then, that there are teachers and leaders with great expertise in pedagogy but are too afraid to share their talent with their teammates or other teachers.

Just as an abundance of confidence helps people take risks and tackle large projects, a confidence deficit can serve as an inhibitor. In some cases, this can lead to work avoidance. A lack of confidence and self-esteem also negatively affects educators before they even enter the workforce. Lois Frankel (2004) has noted that people with low self-esteem often try to remain under the radar because they don't want to be noticed, but this is the wrong thing to do. To excel in education means we need to do everything possible to help ourselves grow (i.e., mitigate our weaknesses and build upon our strengths) and add value to the organizations and people we serve. Trying to stay unnoticed does not help accomplish either of those goals.

Ability to Self-Monitor and Self-Correct

There is nothing worse than putting time and energy into a project only to receive feedback that it was not satisfactory and you need to begin your efforts anew. This has happened to all of us at some point—either in our careers or personal lives. Thinking back to my dissertation, I cannot count the number of times I wrote what I thought were 12 great pages only to delete them after peer revision or professor feedback. That cycle of starting and stopping eventually grows tiresome and makes starting over more and more difficult. I felt myself wanting just to avoid the work altogether. As I developed and gained more skills, however, I began to notice what I was doing that would ultimately cause me to delete multiple pages of text and start over. As a result, I learned to self-correct.

Over time, the revisions and feedback my peers and professors provided became much less painful, and I did not feel a sense of dread when I sat down to the computer. In other words, my slowly growing desire to avoid doing the work ceased as my ability to self-monitor and self-correct grew. Being able to self-correct means there is a clear understanding of the desired outcome and the best approach to achieving that goal.

In each chapter of this book you will find two recurring sections: Coping Mechanisms and Solutions. The intent of the Coping Mechanisms section is to provide some quick fixes that will help you be more productive and efficient at work, less stressed, and better able to meet deadlines and expectations. This is the aspirin to take care of your symptom—time management—that is growing out of a bigger underlying challenge. The Solutions section helps you look for the cure to that bigger ailment. We will dig deeper into the root causes and provide research-based guidance for addressing more complex problems.

Coping Mechanisms

Eat the big frog first. Mark Twain once said that if the first thing you had to do each day was eat a live frog, then the remaining tasks would seem simple. Nothing could be as bad as that first thing. This concept has been discussed many times over the years and has been popularized by Brian Tracy (2007). Tracy extends Twain's thoughts to discuss the concept of eating the big frog first. Simply stated, if you are faced with an undesirable decision on one hand and a horrific, dreaded decision on the other, make the horrific decision first. After that, the undesirable decision will not seem so bad.

This speaks directly to work avoidance. Do you have an email pinned to the top of your inbox that you still have not acted on? I'm talking to you. Do you have a deadline to meet but are carrying on with other nonessential tasks instead of buckling down and doing the work? I'm talking to you. Eating the big frog first is about understanding that work avoidance does everyone a disservice, especially the one avoiding the work. They put themselves in a lose-lose situation, and the only way out is to eat the big frog.

Make sure your calendar matches your priorities. Nearly everyone I know keeps a calendar of some sort. Some are the pocket variety, some are portfolios, but most people depend on electronic support (e.g., Outlook, Google Calendar) to help them organize their life. However, many people do not take the time to think about, much less write down, what their priorities are. This may seem like a simple task, but it's incredibly important. List your priorities, such as family, friends, faith, profession, and health, in varying combinations and rank order. Then, looking at the big picture, determine whether your schedule matches those priorities. For myself, I know that nowhere on my list of priorities is nonprofessional use of social media, but I know that on a weekly basis (at least), I find myself buried in social media instead of interacting with my wife and kids. I suspect I am not the only one.

Looking through a smaller lens than our overall priorities, we can examine our main concerns professionally. Do we match our calendars (and thus our time) on the areas that have the biggest impact on our overall success? As educators, this boils down to whether we spend the majority of our time working to ensure we are doing everything we can to best serve our students. Taking the time to consider personal priorities is a great place to start better managing our time and ensure we are tackling the most critical and complex tasks that continue to confront us.

Schedule flextime. One of the greatest joys of working on time management skills is the realization that you can, in fact, manage your own time. Taking back control of one major element of your life can serve both to embolden us and encourage growth in other areas. Whether we like to admit it or not, we all have discretionary time built into our crazy schedules. For example, every educator I know, from paraprofessionals to teachers to administrators, says they could do a better job of communicating home—particularly the good news. It is eminently possible to block off a half-hour every two weeks for this sole purpose. In fact, it is possible to do much more than that if we have the courage to take back our calendars and intentionally schedule flex- or discretionary time to focus on priorities and goals.

Personally, I schedule time each week to think. That's right. I sit at my desk and think. Sometimes I read; other times I sit silently. It may seem unproductive, but I have found it to be the most beneficial time I spend each week. I organize my thoughts, focus my actions, and ensure I am working to make progress each day instead of just making it through the day. That concept—attacking the day—is essential to time management. Either you do the work, or the work does you. How you manage your time dictates which direction that battle will go.

Seek out an accountability partner. One of the greatest gifts you can give yourself is the gift of accountability. Let's face it: as humans, we are pretty poor at holding ourselves accountable. There is no better example than physical fitness and health. Science and the media have demystified how to attain (and retain) the physique we want. The knowledge is readily available, and for the vast majority of people, the solution is possible. Still (at least in the United States), we are more overweight than ever before. What gives?

In short, there is a gap between knowledge and execution. That gap is the ability to hold ourselves accountable to our goals. In fact, in some cases, we are so afraid of failing that we will not even publicly admit where we want to be in terms of health and fitness. This is why having someone else hold you accountable is so powerful—nay, necessary. To have an accountability partner means the following things have taken place:

- Goals have been formed.
- Priorities have been established.
- Information has been shared with someone else.
- You have committed to reporting out your progress regularly (ideally, every day since every single day counts).

Accountability partners or coaches are not a new concept. Marshall Goldsmith explores this concept brilliantly in his book *Triggers* (Goldsmith & Reiter, 2015). That book helped me realize that we do our best work when we have shared our goals with someone. The process of sharing goals inherently means we are also sharing something that is meaningful and significant to us. The question for anyone reading this book is whether time management—and specifically work avoidance—is an area you are committed to improving. If so, creating a simple statement (and then reporting out to an accountability partner on your performance) can serve to help lead a transformation in performance. *Today, I did my best to tackle the most complex task facing me first thing in the morning.*

Solutions

This section addresses some of the more common underlying issues that cause time management issues or cause someone to work at less than peak efficiency. Again, this book operates from the paradigm that (in the case of this chapter) time management is not the issue; it is actually a symptom of a deeper problem: work avoidance. Thus, this section provides lasting solutions designed not only for the person experiencing time management issues but also for leaders, coaches, and colleagues who are working to help that person get past his or her issue.

Focus on Skill Acquisition

In the words of Jim Rohn (2003), "Don't wish it was easier, wish you were better. Don't wish for less problems, wish for more skills. Don't wish for less challenge, wish for more wisdom." The primary issue with work avoidance is the self-perceived lack of skill to handle a situation adeptly. Most people do not like to do things they believe they are bad at. There is no sense of validation—only increased stress and frustration. Thus, instead of completing tasks, we avoid them, either hoping to be forgiven or waiting to the point where we no longer have a choice but to get the task completed. Though there is not just one universal solution for how to acquire new skills, the following tips and techniques might be good places to start.

Seek out honest feedback. Most people will be able to easily identify what their skill deficiency is and what is holding them back from both a higher level of production and a lower level of stress. They may identify the symptoms and not the cause—as discussed throughout this book—but most have an idea. Thus, the first person from whom you should seek honest feedback is yourself. If you truly do not have an idea what the skill deficiency may be, it's time to ask for help or support. This does not mean you are unaware or ignorant; it simply means you have a blind spot when it comes to a specific area (or areas) of your abilities and performance. We all have blind spots in different aspects of our lives, and seeking help from a trusted friend, colleague, or mentor can help you to identify exactly where you can best spend your time to improve your craft.

Accrue your 10,000 hours. The 10,000-hour rule is often attributed to psychologist and best-selling author Malcolm Gladwell (2008). The rule asserts that deliberate practice at anything for 10,000 hours leads to the possibility of performing at an expert level. Some newer studies have found that this may not be the case, and deliberate practice leads to improved performance in nondynamic settings. Regardless of what you believe, the bottom line is that you cannot achieve mastery of a skill or subject without putting in the time. Therefore, one of the best things you can do if skill deficiencies are leading to work avoidance is dedicate the time to simply do the work. Over time, this may be the best possible way to increase your own skills and performance.

Hone Your Grit

Grit is the ability to recognize an initial setback or struggle and persevere beyond it. Researcher Angela Duckworth (2016) is doing tremendous work shining a light on grit and the effect it has on our students, but it is just as important to study and understand for the adults in our building. Grit is not something that can be taught in a workshop and then immediately implemented. It is bigger than that; it involves a philosophical and mindset shift for most people. It taps into our ability to have self-efficacy, but it also provides direction that helps us not only believe we can be great but also push through obstacles prohibiting us from obtaining our performance objectives. You either think your way into new behavior, or you behave your way into a new way of thinking. When it comes to grit, we must think ourselves into it. We can do this in several ways, but at the end of the day, you must want to learn about grit (in your preferred modality) in order to change your behavior.

Train the trainer. Grit has a definitive place in schools. Duckworth's research has identified grit as a better predictor of future success than GPA and other highly regarded metrics (2016). A great way for adults to better learn about grit and work to embody the characteristics of someone with grit and a growth mindset is to teach the material. Giving your teachers a solid foundation in concepts around grit and encouraging them to pass that knowledge on to their students helps foster a spirit of "grittiness" in a building that can energize and motivate. Ultimately, this can serve to have a very positive effect on those who typically exhibit work avoidance.

Identify negative language and work to reframe problems. In *Above the Line: Lessons in Leadership and Life from a Championship Season* (Meyer & Coffey, 2015), the authors identify a language pattern commonly used when substandard performance is prevalent. This pattern is referred to as BCD behavior. People first *blame* others, then *complain* about the circumstances, and then *defend* their position. For instance, "I didn't get the lesson plans because I know the principal never even reads them anyway. The fact they want them every week is ridiculous, particularly when I am so busy providing interventions. What is more important anyway?" BCD language is prevalent in work avoiders and serves to foster the status quo. Teaching people about this language pattern, and providing a tool for immediate self–monitoring, helps eliminate this behavior and promote behaviors more centered around grit.

A tool to move forward can be to implement TCO language as the converse to BCD language. TCO language asks for the objective *truth*, the *conditions* of the situation, and the *ownership* of the situation. Using the example above, it might look like this: "The lesson plans weren't turned in on time. I struggle to find the value in this task as I have never received feedback on what has been turned in. Still, I knew the expectation and should have met that standard." The key to TCO language is the conditions section. This allows people to voice their displeasure or rationale for the behavior, but the final step is still asking them to own their personal decisions and behavior.

Give the time. Like it or not, grit takes time. It may not seem self-evident that a book centered on better time management would promote something that is going to take a large chunk of time, but making space now to develop grit will ultimately save time and stress in the future. The ability to fight through an obstacle without having to stop, rethink, and potentially quit will save a great amount of time over the long term.

Align Your Priorities

As discussed in the introductory example with Danny, work avoidance often occurs when priorities don't match assigned tasks or required work. In these cases, difficult internal dialogue must take place. First, the decision either to lead or to comply must be made. If you truly believe that the work assigned to you does not lead your organization toward its mission, then you must care enough to lead a conversation about reconfiguring the tactics put in place to best achieve that goal. If you cannot argue or debate the rationale behind the work being done, and you would just prefer to do it a different way (i.e., your way), then it is time to comply. If working toward alignment through leadership or being complicit are not steps you are willing to take, the best you can hope for is to remedy the symptoms of your time management issue because they will never cease. Remember, while it seems like you are "choosing you" by refusing to create alignment in your own life, it will ultimately be *you* that loses by taking on additional stress and strife.

Gain Confidence

Confidence allows us to take risks and believe that we are capable of more today than we were yesterday—and to have abundant hope for tomorrow. Simply stated, confidence means we believe we are capable, and for the most part, we become what we think about for ourselves. As a result, confidence allows us to tackle difficult tasks and not avoid work that in the past may have been considered too much, too hard, or too time-consuming.

Engage in self-talk. Many people are their own worst critic. Nonstop nagging and self-hate spews inside our brains as a constant form of self-talk. Turning off this destructive mechanism is the first step to moving forward and building confidence. Take the time to consciously think about your thinking, and make a conscious effort to eliminate negative self-talk. This will put you on the road to building lasting confidence.

Build up personal compassion. Compassion is widely held as a desired characteristic, but its meaning (and whether it can be measured) is still hotly debated and discussed. A recent study attempted to better describe this abstract concept through five components: recognizing suffering; understanding its universality; feeling sympathy, empathy, or concern for those who are suffering (i.e., emotional resonance); tolerating the associated distress; and acting to alleviate the suffering (Strauss et al., 2016). Although this is a broad concept to consider, feeling compassion for one's self while working through work avoidance issues is paramount to creating lasting change and building confidence.

Abandon concepts of perfection. The desire for perfection often inhibits progress. Progress, not perfection, is the goal. Education is an extraordinarily human profession. Every single input and output is human—and therefore volatile. The perfect school will never be constructed, nor will there ever be a perfect teacher or school leader. Therefore, perfection should never be the goal. The pursuit of perfection is doomed to fail and provide another blow to the confidence of someone who may already be struggling to maintain confidence and self-esteem.

Serve others. Those struggling with confidence often place an inordinate amount of importance on what others think about them (or what they think others think about them). Serving others, therefore, provides multiple distinct benefits. First, the act of being kind and serving others is just universally a good idea. Other benefits come from building positive relationships and building others' confidence in you as a peer, colleague, and leader. Additionally, working through someone else's problem is often less daunting for many and does not involve the same ego or confidence if something goes awry. For instance, I was coaching an assistant principal who was stagnant in his current job, but he wasn't confident enough to explore new opportunities. His best friend happened to be going through an extensive interview process with a distinguished district. After helping his friend with the interview preparation process, he realized just how ready he was to take the next step in his own career. By serving someone else, he was able to build his own confidence to chase down his dreams.

Engage in Self-Monitoring

Earlier in this chapter, we discussed the inability to self-monitor or self-correct as a sign that you may be work avoidant. In order to move past work-avoidant tendencies, a direct emphasis must be made on improving our ability to self-monitor, which is the ability to respond appropriately to societal and professional cues as guidelines for behaviors. An underlying factor to keep in mind is the notion that understanding who you really are is key to allowing you to become the person you ultimately want to be.

Understand how self-monitoring offers clarity and control. No lasting change will help those who suffer from work avoidance until they feel a semblance of control over their environment. Many people feel that, within their job and life, they are data rich but information poor. This adds to their feelings of powerlessness. Having the right kinds of data helps establish a sense of control within your work environment, so go beyond merely monitoring and tracking school data to gather valuable data about your own habits. For example, getting a true understanding of exactly how much time you spend working with kids, compared to what you see as cumbersome paperwork, may expose many truths about your performance versus your perception.

Create an environment that rewards self-regulation. Work avoidant people benefit from an environment that rewards self-regulation. What exactly does that mean? Environments that are not static and allow and promote critical thought and innovation help to support work-avoidant people by allowing them to feel as though they can fail forward without retribution. One way a school leader can do this is by providing "Feel Free to Fail" cards. I borrowed this idea from a neighboring superintendent in my area. As a principal, I hand out these cards at the beginning of each year and ask that when teachers try something new—that does not work—they come in and talk to me about it. I always thank them for being innovative and then return the card to them about a week later and tell them to keep going. This is just one quick example of what leaders can do to promote a risk-taking environment that is safe for their faculty and staff. People will not take risks if they do not feel safe and supported.

Foster positive work relationships. People, not policies or programs, make great organizations. In any line of work, people are willing and able to perform brilliant tasks when others see them for what they can be—not for what they are. Many leaders tend to demand and demean when people do not meet deadlines and seem work avoidant. Accountability in any industry or line of work is a must, but if taking a hard line isn't changing outcomes for someone who is work avoidant, it is important to look at the problem in a different way. Work-avoidant people are often fearful of making mistakes, so providing them with a safe place to work and potentially fail (or succeed) is imperative to helping them move forward with increased efficiency and engagement in the workplace.

Final Thoughts

Work-avoidant people are not lazy. It is an indolent narrative of leaders to write off their work-avoidant staff as such, and it's a sign of a self-negating mindset when someone assigns themselves that label. More important, such a label does nothing to help correct the behavior. If you find yourself or someone you work with or lead as work avoidant, work to improve their skills, grit, self-confidence, and ability to self-correct. Additionally, understand that making strides and progress in these areas is not easy or quick. This is a process of acquiring skills and growing as a person and professional. The bad news is that this is precise and legitimately difficult work. The good news is that cutting back on work-avoidant behaviors to become more productive is eminently doable. In the next chapter, we'll look at one of the most difficult challenges around time management: pleasing others.

2

People Pleaser

Every person reading this book has immediately reacted to a request from a boss or coworker by saying *yes* without thinking twice. The person making the request says a quick *thank you*, provides cursory instructions, and walks away. Then you sit at your desk and think, "What in the world have I just gotten myself into?" Sound familiar? Most people learn from this experience and in time become more judicious when volunteering for activities or accepting undue responsibility. Others seemingly never learn and continue to struggle through their personal and professional lives constantly saying *yes* to everyone but themselves. These are the people pleasers, and this chapter is for them.

Brandon is your prototypical people pleaser. Brandon serves as the director of technology for a medium-sized district and manages a department of 10 people and well over 5,000 devices. I first met Brandon in a leadership meeting for his district. These meetings look different in every district, but in Brandon's district, all principals and department leaders gathered once a month with their superintendent to review operations and discuss different leadership topics. The meeting went smoothly, and of the

14 people around the table, Brandon definitely stood out among the crowd. He was quick-witted, outgoing, and seemed to serve as the de facto leader of all department heads.

As my work continued with the district and I learned more about the dynamics of the group, it became clear there was more to Brandon and his performance than what I had gleaned from our initial meeting. As I met with leader after leader to discuss the state of the district, it became more and more apparent that Brandon's department was underdelivering on many promises. To be clear, it was not a poor-performing department when measurables were evaluated or examined from an outside eye. However, almost every other leader felt let down in some way by Brandon and his team. How could this happen? The department was doing well, yet others felt let down by their colleague?

In addition, Brandon was exhausted when I met with him. He explained that he was a father of five and had extensive civic and faith-based responsibilities outside his work in the district. He felt he was always on the go and that the responsibilities of a department head, father, and contributing member of the community were potentially more than any one person could handle. Simply put, Brandon was at the absolute end of his line.

I asked Brandon to make a list of everything that was "hanging over his head" at work and still needed to be done. Brandon quickly put together a list of about 20 items. I asked him to categorize the work according to building or department. He did so, and it was apparent that the work was pretty evenly distributed throughout the district. I then had him check his outstanding list of items to do against the outstanding work orders in the district's software system. There were massive differences. When I asked him why this was the case, he explained that these were projects that individuals had asked him to work on at one point in time. When I asked him if those projects were important, he replied that they must be important to *them*. I asked if they were important to the goals of the district, and he admitted that he had not even thought about it that way.

With Brandon's permission, I asked the other directors and principals to comment directly on Brandon as a coworker. Almost universally, his colleagues commented on Brandon's performance by first explaining how great of a guy he is and how much they love him as a person. They continued by saying that he has no follow-through and cannot be trusted to do his job. A handful of coworkers went on to explain that if he weren't such a great guy, he would be collectively disliked as a result of being so unreliable.

When I shared this information with Brandon, I asked him why he thinks this might be the case. Brandon quickly self-identified, "I never say *no*. I say *yes* to projects I know I won't get to and then the work just builds. It is like this is a never-ending cycle." Once Brandon self-identified, it was easy to work him through the next steps (as we will do throughout this chapter). It is important to note, however, that Brandon was in the midst of the worst possible fate of the people pleaser. He had attempted to please so many people that he began to let others down, *and* the people-pleasing behavior had led to struggles in his personal life. If you are operating as a people pleaser, this may not be where you are currently, but it will almost certainly be your ultimate fate unless you have a superhuman capacity combined with great individual project efficiency. Let Brandon's situation serve as a cautionary tale.

Job Descriptions

Nobody knows your job description entirely except for you and your immediate supervisor. Even though most organizations have a collection of job descriptions filled with jargon and lawyer-speak, these documents certainly do not tell the whole story of what takes place between the start and end of your work day. So, almost nobody (literally) with whom you work truly understands the scope of all you do for your school and your students. This is true for administrative assistants, teachers, custodians, food service workers, and so on and so forth.

The reason I feel compelled to include this section here is simple: nobody really knows the challenges and struggles that come along with your unique situation. This is meant both to empower you and to provide some context for sympathy—and perhaps empathy—to enter the equation. I see this so often in my district and in other districts where I work. What we want for ourselves, we too often neglect to give others.

In the previous scenario, Brandon may have felt compelled to always say *yes* to every request because he did not want people to think he was lazy. However, the principals and other directors making those requests most likely had no idea how many work orders were submitted daily or how many "special" projects the superintendent may have had him working on.

This is the point. People pleasers typically assume that others are far busier or more overwhelmed than they are, and they end up just barely treading water because they cannot manage their time appropriately or efficiently complete tasks. If you are still unsure if you are a people pleaser or not, the next section will run through some telltale signs in greater detail before we start to work toward some solutions.

Signs You Are a People Pleaser

People-pleasing actions are generally a manifestation of one of two core drivers of behavior: the desire to avoid conflicts or the desire to build relationships as the preeminent goal of employment. Based on this description, if you cannot self-identify or are uncomfortable self-identifying, this section will explore tangible behaviors that serve as symptoms of people-pleasing behavior.

You Are Delegated To (A LOT)

When someone trusts you with an important project, it can almost be intoxicating. It is flattering to think that someone trusts you with an important task and that you—instead of your colleagues—were chosen to help work toward a specific outcome. Delegation also feeds our innate desire to have control over things and influence over others and projects. These are natural reactions. In addition, being intentionally delegated to by a supervisor or peer can mean great things. It may mean they value your work, see untapped potential, and want to involve you in major initiatives or projects. With that in mind, this section should not alarm you if you are the one being delegated to by peers or supervisors.

However, if you are repeatedly given tasks that are menial, time-consuming, not increasing in complexity, or have not built your personal capacity, then some red flags should be raised. In essence, if people are pushing work they should be doing on to you without a productive end in sight, then they are not valuing your time. They have redefined your job description to include whatever work they give you. In some cases, this is just part of the job. In other cases, they are giving suboptimal tasks to you because you refuse to challenge them on why the task is best suited for your skills. If you feel as though you are consistently given tasks that are not helping you grow or are not specific to your role or capacity, then it may be a sign that you are viewed as a people pleaser and are (in a sense) being used as a result of your inability to self-advocate.

You Never Say *No*

Here are two quick mental tests I would like you to give yourself. First, when was the last time you said *no* when somebody asked you to do something? This includes your personal life and can extend to a friend asking you to help move or to your mother asking you to do something (that she would not even think to ask your siblings). If you are having a hard time coming up with a time, then you may be a people pleaser.

Second, when was the last time you agreed to do something and regretted it before the words even left your mouth? For example, let's say you have your first Saturday free in five weeks, and your colleague asks if you will help supervise the 8th grade community service project—despite the fact that your school only serves PreK through 2nd grade—and you still say *yes*!

It is true that saying *yes* and helping others isn't inherently a bad thing. In fact, it is a great thing. It is something that our society depends on, and it's a great attribute to model for students. However, when you become someone's crutch or—even worse—an organization's crutch, helping out can be a bad thing for everyone involved. It is unhealthy for an organization or a relationship to be singularly dependent on one individual, and it is nearly impossible to be productive and satisfied as a human being if you are continually working on someone else's behalf.

Remember this: It is great to be of service and to support and help others. But saying *yes* and doing someone else's work does not necessarily make you of true service to that person or the organization.

You Are Delegated To (Again)

I refused to delegate when I became a principal. I am a reformed people pleaser, and I vividly remember the long evenings and Saturday afternoons of duty completed during my 20s. I vowed to myself that I would not do to others what was done to me. Six months into my job as a high school principal, I found myself working incomprehensible hours and never feeling as though I could get ahead of the curve. Then, in passing one day, my boss asked me who I was working to grow in my building. I went through a laundry list of teachers, and when I was finished, he asked how I was developing them. I replied that I was using observation and feedback. He nodded affirmatively and commended my efforts. I am not sure if at that point I was actually sticking my chest out feeling proud or not, but I was certainly thinking along those lines. Then came the crushing question: "What else are you doing?" I stammered, searching for an answer, and he just kept waiting.

The people pleaser in me wanted so badly to find the right answer to satisfy my boss. Finally, somewhat defeated, I told him I was not sure I was doing anything else. He went through a list of items accomplished (to-dos) that I was turning into him as part of my monthly report and asked why others in the building could not complete some of that work. I started to explain to him my (somewhat radical) philosophy on delegation. He then asked if I was against giving people additional work or against people growing. I of course answered with the former. He explained that I should think of delegation from a growth perspective. If someone could grow from it, then it wasn't simply busywork. If, however, nobody could get better or grow as a result of the task, then I should evaluate if it was best done by me or the office staff. If the task was actually best done by me, then (and only then) I should continue to grind through the work.

This coaching conversation was incredibly poignant for me. It was in that moment that I realized my lack of delegation was both an attempt to people please and selfish at the exact same time. If you are still questioning whether you are a people pleaser, evaluate your actions and ask one simple question: *Have I delegated any work in the last week?* If you have owned everything that's come across your desk, then chances are good that you are more of a people pleaser than you think.

Coping Mechanisms

Just say *no.* There is power in saying *no*. Ideally, this is not done arbitrarily, but even if it is? So be it. There are many variations that the people pleaser can try. Some may be a little softer;

some may be a little harsher—but what matters most is getting practice in saying *no*. Here are a few phrases to practice until you get to the point where you can easily say *no* to others:

- If I take that on, I am afraid it will negatively affect me achieving our stated goal.
- I am swamped right now. Can you get help from somebody else?
- I won't be able to get to this for a couple weeks. Is this something you need immediately?
- This work isn't of particular interest to me.

These are merely a few of the many alternatives you can use to just say *no*. When you're first getting used to the concept of saying *no*, you may possess a strong desire to do so via email (to avoid conflict). This is not the preferred mechanism to deliver this news. Particularly during the learning stage, as you try to progress forward from definitive people-pleasing tendencies, it is important to get outside your comfort zone and engage in face-to-face interaction to share this message. Understand that your instinct will be to sugarcoat this message with a plethora of excuses and apologies. Avoid this type of banter at all costs. You belaboring the point of saying *no* does not make anyone feel better about the situation. This discourse serves only one person. It is for you and you alone, and progress will be easier if you can discontinue this practice.

If you think this is hard, keep in mind the work of Jia Jiang (2016). In his TED talk, Jiang explains that he was terrified of rejection, so he set out to force himself into situations of rejection for 100 straight days. This is *a lot* harder than just saying *no*. As a result, Jiang learned three essential lessons that also feed into our exercise of saying *no* and trying not to be a people pleaser:

- Fear supersedes the reality of what happens when we say or are told *no*.

- The humanity of the other people involved will be revealed when we finally say *no*.
- Relationships can emerge and improve through this exercise.

The world of rejection is a place where the fears from such snubs are much more destructive than the actual rejection. Thankfully, we have the ability to make rejection less painful than we believed it would be, and we can restore our faith in humanity knowing that people are much kinder than we ever imagined.

The connection between Jiang's work and the practice of saying *no* exists in the last sentence. Most people who are burdening people pleasers with additional tasks and work are not inherently bad people. The practice of saying *no* and engaging in respectful dialogue in a majority of circumstances will serve to improve your relationships, not destroy them.

Ask for time. If you read the above and froze since you are currently incapable of having a direct conversation with someone and informing them that you cannot do whatever task they decided to make part of your job description, you're in luck. There is a less direct first step you can take. Simply ask for some time to consider your response before agreeing to take on the work. If even this is too direct, asking for time to consult your schedule and see if it's possible to complete the task or assignment in a timely manner is another variation of the same concept. The best-case scenario is that the delegator will simply move on to the next potential people pleaser, and you avoided the task without even having to say *no*. If he or she does not move on, then the requested time at least gives you the opportunity to mentally prepare for letting someone down. You can practice the conversation and recommit to the internal strength to choose productivity and purpose over pleasing someone else.

Determine who benefits most. I had to hang a sign in my office when I was learning to say *no* that said, "Who benefits most by doing this work?" I had become so accustomed to being the hero (in my eyes) and being great at completing tasks that I needed an artificial reminder to help me learn to delegate. If you are a people pleaser and struggle with time management, you may also need this type of support. To be honest, I needed more than just the sign. As principal, I wanted to systematize our annual calendar. I wanted to know exactly what things should be done in October, December, April, and so forth, so I logged all major occurrences and work items that needed to be accomplished. I eventually had to add two columns to this spreadsheet. One column stated who completed or led each action, and the other stated who would benefit most by completing the work. In essence, I had to create a system in which I gave myself permission to not complete work that was best completed by my colleagues.

An auxiliary benefit of the who-benefits-most mentality is that it can easily be used in conversations with colleagues and supervisors who may have grown dependent on you for completing work that is best completed by them or someone else. This simple question changes the dynamic of the conversation and can provide even the most deeply entrenched people pleaser an alternative to simply saying *no*.

Solutions

Although the coping mechanisms offered in the previous section should lead to increased productivity, the bottom line is that the problem has not been solved. To reiterate the analogy used in the introduction, those mechanisms are simply aspirin treating a more complex disease. They may provide some immediate relief from the symptoms, but the only way long-term success can be achieved is by putting in the work to shift your thinking. New ways of thinking lead to new ways of behaving. This is difficult work, but it is possible!

Identify Your Purpose

In *The Purpose-Driven Life*, Richard Warren (2002) emphasizes that the most precious gift any of us has is time. The challenge for each of us is to figure out how to best use the time allotted us to maximize our lives both personally and professionally. Ideally, if we make better use of our time, it will make us not only more efficient and effective but also happier and more content.

Why does your job exist? I am willing to guess that nobody reading this book is employed simply to make another adult's life easier, nor were you employed to stay in your office all day and complete paperwork. Educators and school leaders are put in place to run complex organizations so they may best serve student needs. As agents of those institutions, our jobs (though incredibly complex) are to do whatever we can to best serve our students and communities. Working to identify the purpose of why your particular job exists will help clarify whether the work you are spending your time on is purposeful and adds meaning and true value to your organization. It is vital for leaders of educational institutions to remember that at the very core level, the job of an educational leader is to create a system that produces more leaders—not more followers.

Identify when you are most happy. Happiness is complex and an interesting word to include in this section, but it is used intentionally. I choose to explore happiness as a construct because despite being well researched, it is abundantly misunderstood. A pioneer in the field of positive psychology, Dr. Martin Seligman identified an acronym—PERMA—that stands for the five key elements that comprise well-being and are explored in his book *Flourish* (2013):

- **Positive Emotion:** Peace, gratitude, satisfaction, pleasure, inspiration, hope, curiosity, and love fall into this category.
- **Engagement:** This is when we lose ourselves to a task or project that provides us with a sense of "disappeared time" because we are so highly engaged.

- **Relationships:** People who have meaningful, positive relationships with others are happier than those who do not.
- **Meaning:** Meaning comes from serving a cause bigger than
  ourselves. Whether it's a religion or a cause that helps
  humanity in some way, we all need meaning in our lives.
- **Accomplishment/Achievement:** To feel significant life satisfaction, we must strive to better ourselves in some way.

With PERMA in mind, consider when you are most happy
and content at work. Examples among my closest colleagues
range from when they are observing instruction, to playing with
data, to having face-to-face conversations, to researching topics
individually. There is no right or wrong answer, but it is important that you can self-identify when you are most happy at work
and then work to steer your job description in that direction if
at all possible.

Align purpose with happiness. I want you to create a
chart like the one in Figure 2.1 to identify alignment with and
gaps between the purpose you bring to work, what you spend
time doing, and what makes you most happy. When there is
alignment among these three key factors, work productivity
will significantly increase. When there is a misalignment, work
performance and productivity will suffer. People pleasers often
spend an inordinate amount of time completing tasks they don't
enjoy or that don't add value to the organization.

Figure 2.1 shows a teacher leader with people-pleasing tendencies. Once daily behaviors are charted, it is clear to see why
this individual may be feeling angst with the growing mountain
of work being heaped on her. The chart may seem hyperbolic,
but it is the life that many emerging leaders live. Tasks are given
in abundance to help prepare them for a future in administrative life. The people pleaser takes on the tasks they find joyless,
which leads to decreased productivity in the areas they care
about—and often truly matter more.

Figure 2.1

Purpose Versus Happiness

Purpose of Job	Common Behaviors and/or Tasks Completed at Work	Behaviors That Provide the Most Happiness
To serve students and help my school achieve its mission of serving the whole child	• Teach my assigned classes. • Complete compliance work on requisitions in the office. • Meet with any student failing a course during my prep period. • Run a report for my principal letting him/her know when teachers last updated their gradebooks. • Monitor the electronic platform for completion of mandatory trainings.	• Anything with kids • Learning how to lead

Focus on Healthy Relationships

People pleasers will not simply read this chapter and swing back to focusing on themselves first and not prioritizing the needs or opinions of others. Nor should they. There are strengths and characteristics within people pleasers that are both admirable and desirable. Thus, people pleasers should not focus on becoming someone else; they should simply focus on forming and maintaining healthy relationships.

The University of Washington (2014) is a leader in defining the characteristics of healthy relationships. They consider the following traits of a healthy, productive relationship: mutual respect, trust, honesty, support, fairness, and effective communication. It is difficult for anyone—even the staunchest people pleaser—to argue that these are not desirable characteristics of a work or personal relationship. The issue for people pleasers is that they often do what is best for others and fail to communicate openly and honestly about the fairness and equity in their relationships. Harboring these thoughts leads to discontentment and resentment. Ultimately, a relationship rooted in these characteristics will almost certainly not be able to endure.

Thus, a relationship based on one party constantly trying to please a second party will rarely succeed. As the relationship progresses and time passes, the people pleaser will continue to do more and more to please his or her colleague, boss, or partner, and the stress and feeling of suffocation will continue to mount as the workload and responsibilities continue to build. If you truly are a people pleaser, then the best possible thing you can do for yourself—*and those you are trying to please*—is to draw a line in the sand and focus on forming healthy, communicative relationships that have the possibility of endurance.

Clarify Your Vision

How great do you see yourself? Most people pleasers have difficulty imagining themselves as greater than they currently are because they are too busy working on carrying out someone else's dream instead of chasing their own. Working concretely on articulating a personal vision for yourself is a key step to opening your eyes to your own potential and to quit living your life's mission to serve someone else's goals and desires.

Vision helps you become a leader in your own life, and a concrete vision creates energy, endurance, and focus for anybody who is pursuing his or her life's passion. My personal vision is to change the world of education so no student is forced to endure an education in 2028 like the one provided in 2018. This is big and audacious, but it gives me the strength I need to say *no* to opportunities that may be fun and exciting but would ultimately distract from the vision I have established for myself.

Depersonalize

Too often, people pleasers forget they do not work for individuals; they work for organizations. In a school setting, we work for the taxpayers of our district or the customer segments that fund our private schools. This is vitally important for people pleasers to remember. Please take these words as permission to say *no*. You *do not* work for Principal Skinner; you work for the Springfield School District. The people we should be focused on pleasing are the kids and the community we serve—not our direct supervisor.

This conscious effort to depersonalize the work we do is incredibly important. It shifts our thinking and empowers us to say *no* to marginal tasks that do not work directly toward satisfying our mission, vision, and goals. Additionally, it is important to depersonalize the work in terms of ego. It feels good to be depended on and valued, and that good feeling is a gateway drug for being a people pleaser. We must also realize that while being needed (both personally and professionally) is nice, it should not define who we are. It is up to each of us to determine how we want to be defined and remembered and then chart our own path toward that goal. If we fail to do so, we will continue to grind away on the job description that others have created for us and continue to be buried beneath a mountain of work. It's time to start living the life you are entitled to and deserve.

Final Thoughts

People pleasers are typically wonderful friends and valued employees. The issue is that they are often living the life of a duck. They look calm and cool on the surface but are working like crazy to stay afloat when you are able to see just below the water line. The work of a people pleaser is simply not sustainable, nor is it healthy for an institution. The great news is that by empowering people pleasers to focus on healthy relationships instead of simply pleasing others, radical change is possible. That change will not only help the individual making the transformation but also serve to better prepare and develop the entire workforce.

3

Prisoner of the Moment

To give you a behind-the-scenes look at the construction of this book, imagine me furiously typing away during the winter break trying to make the best possible use of my time while the majority of the adults and students I serve are not in the building. I am in deep creative thought about how to communicate to my readers how they should drive their decisions around maximizing their time. Things are rolling, and it looks like it is going to be an amazingly productive day.

DING!

DING!

My Twitter alerts started going bananas. One ding led to another, which led to another, which led to another. On its surface, this was a good thing. I had written a blog that was getting shared and was receiving a great deal of feedback, particularly via Twitter. I looked up and realized over an hour had passed. I had to laugh at the irony. The guy writing a book on time management became so distracted that he lost a decent chunk of a day set aside for writing.

I walked out to my assistant and begrudgingly handed her my phone. She knows this drill as it happens about once every six weeks. She questioned, "Can't concentrate today, huh?" I sheepishly smiled and walked away.

This happens to all of us—or at least it does to every person I know. Even those who are incredibly productive can occasionally get side-tracked by unimportant, nonurgent tasks of the day. This doesn't make us bad people or bad employees; it just happens. Which is why before the NCAA basketball tournament each year, dozens of articles are written about lost productivity. By some accounts, $1.3 billion (yes, billion with a *b*) is lost because of reduced productivity during the tournament (Barrabi, 2018).

Simply put, we all get distracted.

However, some people get distracted a lot. You know who I mean. It might be you, it might be a coworker, but you know the person. They often call themselves out as a defense mechanism and cite adult ADHD, or they joke and yell "Squirrel!" once they have been found out for not being able to stay on task. This chapter is designed with those individuals in mind.

Attention Is a Finite Resource

One of the best pieces of advice I have ever received from a coach or mentor is this: only touch a piece of paper once. Not only does this increase efficiency, it also provides implicit pressure to focus deeply on each work item while it is at hand. Complete the task, move forward, and grind toward a new task or goal. Failure to do so leads to attention and decision fatigue— which ultimately leads to decreased productivity. Thanks to this coaching and years of intentional practice (literally), the practice of touching each piece of paper only once and focusing with precision while holding that paper is burned into me as I work through the tasks of the day.

Through my experience coaching and working with countless administrators, I've discerned that prisoners of the moment work themselves through a circle of work. They spend five minutes on task A, twelve minutes on task B, five minutes on task C, six more on task A, and then seventeen minutes on task D. Forty-five minutes later, nothing is done. Pressure—usually self-imposed—is continually mounting, and in that time, two new tasks and one crisis have been added to the to-do list. Nevertheless, a key characteristic of prisoners of the moment is that they are usually intrigued by and compelled to work on the crisis and new tasks. They bring with them a fresh challenge and a renewed energy.

Although this stimulus might seem appealing at the time, the brain is getting more and more fatigued, and, ultimately, it is getting trained to reward the distractions that exist in our workplace. Work becomes more scattered. Progress is slower. Pressure mounts. This is the crux of decision fatigue, which refers to the deteriorating quality of decisions made by an individual after a long session of decision making (Tierney, 2011).

By the end of the day, week, or whatever time interval you want to apply, many things have been started yet relatively few things have been finished. The prisoner of the moment is constantly working—working hard!—but is getting very little done. He or she is in perpetual motion but accomplishes very little in a timely fashion, and most of it is not up to the highest quality they have the potential to produce.

The point here is that prisoners of the moment typically work very hard. They do not choose to be distracted and constantly jump from task to task, but attention spans are finite and the more we continue to jump from task to task, the more we train our brains that the practice is normal. It is a cycle that perpetuates itself unless we intentionally choose to intervene. We have the ability (in most circumstances) to critically think ourselves through the process and make incremental improvements to our efficiency and effectiveness.

Signs You Are a Prisoner of the Moment

Prisoners of the moment desire excitement and energy in their life. Whatever's next and new has the potential to be better than the current state—and therefore deserves to be explored. A prisoner of the moment is the type of person who clicks on an email about a great travel deal and actually follows through and takes an impromptu trip to Cancun. Prisoners of the moment are curious, energetic, and most comfortable in a world that provides them autonomy and the ability to explore.

New Tasks Legitimately Excite You

If you can hardly contain yourself when you come back from a conference, you may be a prisoner of the moment. If you modify a lesson simply because you clicked on a great infographic you discovered while following #edchat, you may be a prisoner of the moment.

Prisoners of the moment are typically anti–status quo and not only believe that better options are always available but also believe that options that may yield similar results are worth exploring simply for the experience. Prisoners of the moment, when they ascend to leadership levels, often classify themselves as visionaries. They love to imagine what could be, but they gain little pleasure from actually doing the work.

This often leads to a point of reckoning where they simply have too many things occurring simultaneously to do any of them well. When this happens, they have a hard time redoubling their efforts on the task that is most important. Instead, they tend to sink their teeth into the task that is going to be the most enjoyable for them to complete. This means the most important tasks are often left incomplete, or they are completed with the least amount of time and energy—thus creating stress and the feeling that time is managing them, instead of the opposite.

Whoever Gets to You Last Wins

The prisoner of the moment may be branded as someone who plays favorites. This behavior manifests in several ways, but the issue here is that the prisoner of the moment may not be giving preferential treatment to "favorite" employees. Instead, in the prisoner of the moment's world, it's whoever gets there last who wins.

Let me explain. If five people ask for five favors, the prisoner of the moment is likely to say *yes* to all five of them but only act on the last request or on the request that best fits his or her idea of an engaging task. As a result, four other people are left disappointed and wondering why their requests were not honored while someone else's was. Quite often, this had nothing to do with the people making the request. Rather, it had everything to do with a desire to operate with autonomy on a task that was deemed exciting.

It's also worth pointing out that whatever task a prisoner of the moment happens to be working on at the time (albeit brief) is usually the most important thing in the world to him or her for that moment, and any attempt to dissuade that mindset offends their desire to be autonomous. So, even though prisoners of the moment have no intention or premeditation of playing favorites, they often behave in a manner that suggests they do. Thus, the reputation persists.

You Have a Deep Desire for Engagement

Prisoners of the moment are not afraid of work. In fact, they love working. They particularly love working on whatever they want to at any given time. This, however, is not always the same task. Trying to maximize the effectiveness of a prisoner of the moment is not as simple as finding what he is passionate about and letting him move with enthusiasm toward that end.

This is because a prisoner of the moment will seek to engage with whatever new task is put in front of him. You see, there is a chance that the new task is better than the old task, so it is undoubtedly worth exploring. To take this out of the realm of work, I encourage you to think back to your days as a college student.

You and a group of six of your closest friends head out for a night on the town. You head to a neighborhood establishment and find it crowded with friends and strangers. You are able to get a table and soon you are talking, laughing, and dancing the night away. Then, seemingly out of nowhere, one person in your group announces that he or she wants to move on to the next bar. Even after your group begrudgingly agrees, the pattern continues at several other places. By the end of the night, you have truly bar hopped around town because one person was never satisfied. And, frustratingly, the first place usually ended up being the most fun anyway.

What does this have to do with prisoners of the moment seeking to engage with their tasks? It simply means that no task is ever going to be entertaining enough to keep their attention for an extended period of time. The tasks have to shift and be modified in order to keep their attention. Moreover, if you attempt to confine a prisoner of the moment, it will become unbearable for that person. The search for excitement is fueled with autonomy. Placing strict confines around a prisoner of the moment is like trying to domesticate a beautiful and majestic wild animal.

You Get Lost in Social Media Purgatory

If you are still unsure if you are a prisoner of the moment, check your internet browsing history. If you open Facebook, Snapchat, Twitter, or Instagram more than a dozen times per day for no productive reason (i.e., when you do not have time to), then you might be a prisoner of the moment. If you stay on a particular app or platform for 35 minutes doing nothing, then you are probably a prisoner of the moment.

It's worth noting that the motivation behind this browsing helps define the characteristics of the person engaging in the behavior. If you are bored at work, not challenged, and just wasting time, then obviously your search data may mirror the above, but this is not who I'm talking about. I'm referring to the person who feels compelled to check every platform because of the possibility he or she may be missing something. Recognizing the difference is vital in understanding yourself and others so you can be a more effective leader.

Coping Mechanisms

Write down daily goals. If you are a prisoner of the moment, you already know that goal setting isn't very exciting to you. I recognize that. Prisoners of the moment may enjoy the goal-setting process as an activity, but it often fails to take hold as an accountability structure or mechanism to increase effectiveness. Nevertheless, the process of writing daily goals is a bit different than a once-per-semester workshop or goal-setting directive. Daily goals can be more engaging and serve to establish a daily sense of urgency. Creating daily goals plays into the personality profile of someone who is a prisoner of the moment while simultaneously providing strength and structure to each day, which is necessary in order to cause growth as both a person and an employee.

Finish first. This could seem abundantly obvious, but one of the greatest strategies for growth is simply to complete the work in front of you before moving on to the next task. Touch the paper once. Increase your intensity of focus on a singular task or piece of a larger project, and move forward only after successful completion of the task.

There is no shortage of suggestions about how to achieve this. I've included a few suggestions here about ways to increase focus and productivity and to eliminate the distractions that tarnish productivity:

- Shut your email browser when engaged with other work.
- Organize your calendar around specific tasks.
- Remove social media apps from your phone, or schedule specific social media time.
- Schedule office hours rather than have an open-door policy.
- Leverage an accountability partner to help determine which tasks should get completed when.

Dig deep daily. My 11-year-old son makes the average picky eater look like an ambitious omnivore. He struggles to eat anything outside his limited comfort zone. As a result, he recently made a New Year's resolution to try one new fruit or vegetable every month. This may not sound like much, but he is looking his fear or obstacle in the eye and creating a plan to go directly at it. The prisoner of the moment can do the same thing. Prisoners of the moment struggle to engage deeply with content. They love participating at the top and along the periphery, but they have little desire to dig deep. This hesitancy allows for any possible distraction to pull them from their stated primary purpose. Making a conscious effort to dig deep daily into at least one task—as uncomfortable as it may be—is how they can strengthen this muscle of effectiveness.

Create visual reminders to maintain focus on the most important thing. This one is simple. Get creative or artsy or just write this on a big piece of butcher block paper and hang it somewhere in your classroom or office: *Is this the absolute most important thing I could be working on to achieve my goals?* This visual reminder is as simple as it gets, but it can help rewire the brain by constantly reminding you of what you should be spending your time on.

For those of you who are well versed in self-help and self-development reading, this is a perfect place to recall Dr. Stephen Covey's matrix for *urgent* versus *important* as detailed in

The 7 Habits of Highly Effective People (2004). The matrix places importance on one continuum and urgency on another, thereby creating four quadrants. In the lower-left quadrant, you have urgent but unimportant tasks. These include the constant dings of email and the impromptu walk-in meetings that dominate many days. The upper-left quadrant denotes urgent and important activities. These can best be understood as the true emergencies that arise in day-to-day life. The bottom-right quadrant includes unimportant and nonurgent activities. This is your discretionary time (e.g., Facebook, video games, and so on). The upper-right corner includes tasks that are important but not urgent. This is where Covey suggests that we shift more of our time and effort. This quadrant includes things such as exercise, reflection, and future planning.

Solutions

Seek to Understand Your Brain

Our brains are amazing. The more we think about how we think—often referred to as metacognition—the more we want to know. The brain apparently loves learning about itself. As interesting as it is to learn about the brain, it is abundantly clear as we dig deeply into how our brain acts that it is unmistakably hard to control.

Think about it. You are having a romantic dinner with your spouse and you recall a random story from your youth for a seemingly nonsensical reason. Or you are in a conversation with someone and mentally grind for several minutes trying to think of a mutual friend's name. It's not until two days later on the treadmill that it pops into your head. *Tim Morris! Yes, of course. How could I forget Tim Morris?*

A biological reason for your wandering attention is provided by David Rock in his book *Your Brain at Work* (2009). He notes that the nervous system is always working and demanding your brain do the same. This work involves processing, reconfiguring, and reconnecting the trillions of connections in your brain each moment. This is called ambient neural activity. Have you ever wondered why sometimes you are just as exhausted after a mentally taxing day as you would be from a physically grueling day? This is a key reason why.

I love the way Rock describes this. He asks the reader to imagine the brain as though it were Earth. The electrical activity constantly taking place in the brain is similar to the electrical activity taking place in Earth's atmosphere during a horrific lightning storm. It is frankly amazing that anyone is able to persist through difficult activities, given both the internal and external distractions with which we are constantly surrounded.

Rock cites the work of two neuroscientists, Trey Hedden and John Gabrieli, who note that lapses in attention impair our performance, independent of what the task is. This makes sense, but the science behind it is fascinating because it points to clues about how we can train ourselves to be better at staying focused.

Lapses in attention commonly involve the activation of the medial prefrontal cortex. This part of the brain "turns on" when you think about yourself and other people and when you lose engagement in a task or are not doing much at all. Simply, when your external stimuli do not create focus for you, this part of the brain activates and your attention goes to more internal signals, such as being more aware of something that may be bothering you. In turn, this triggers a lapse in attention and focus and leads to decreased focus and productivity.

Actively working to take control of this behavior and mitigating its negative impact begins by understanding the processes taking place within your own brain. A firm grasp of what is happening when you lose attention and focus can serve as a necessary reminder to reengage with an external task instead of allowing your brain to choose its own adventure.

Train Your Brain

Meditation serves a multitude of health and mental purposes. Belief in these benefits has led to the practice of meditation within and between many cultures and religions for thousands of years. Academia and science have recently taken note, and many studies have been conducted to measure the true impact of meditation. These have ended in almost universally accepted meta-analyses noting its many benefits, including its effect on focus and relationships (Khoury, Sharma, Rush, & Fournier, 2015; Sedlmeier et al., 2012).

According to one extensive review that examined the current state of neuroscience research on mindfulness meditation (Tang, Holzel, & Posner, 2015),

> Although meditation research is still in its infancy, a number of studies have investigated changes in brain activation (at rest and during specific tasks) that are associated with the practice of, or that follow, training in mindfulness meditation. . . . There is emerging evidence that mindfulness meditation might cause neuroplastic changes in the structure and function of brain regions involved in regulation of attention, emotion, and self-awareness. (pp. 213, 222)

Wow! Mindfulness mediation can affect the structure of the brain? This assertion is based on 21 different studies of over 300 brains, and the study found that eight brain regions were consistently altered in the experienced meditators. Per the study, the effect of meditation on these particular brain structures appeared to be similar to the effect size of other behavioral, educational, and psychological interventions.

The study also noted changes in brain activation patterns. In their review, Tang, Holzel, and Posner investigated whether mindfulness meditation exerts its effects via altered activation of brain regions involved with focus and attention. Their findings indicate that mindful meditation helps increase our ability to focus attention and have greater control over where our thoughts go. In essence, the practice of meditation can help us rewire our brains in a way that increases focus and can help move us from the frantic pace and lifestyle dictated by being a prisoner of the moment.

Take Smart Breaks and Track Progress

Remember, attention is a finite resource. Taking breaks intentionally helps refuel the brain so it can start back up on the same task with renewed vigor. Taking a break is not intended to be a break from one sensory demanding task to another, and that includes checking email or social media. A break means a break.

If you want to maximize the effectiveness of the break, then take a walk, do 10 push-ups, and drink a glass of water. Physical activity and hydration are key components of sustaining mental energy and creativity. If you work in an environment that allows it, a true lunchtime workout is a great solution to many problems. Pertaining directly to this chapter, a lunchtime workout serves many purposes. Work in the weight room or on the cardio machine will increase focus and productivity during the second half of the day.

The simple task of forcing yourself to take a break and reflect on how you spent your time between breaks is an important variable for continued improvement. Charting your progress so you can see that during one 75-minute span of work you attacked eight different tasks and completed none of them is just the eye-opener some people need to commit to this change.

Final Thoughts

We are in the midst of an information revolution. We produce and consume more information that at any other time in history. Moreover, the amount of data and information being produced and consumed—and expected to be produced and consumed—continues to increase at nearly exponential rates. The people and organizations competing for our attention are doing so in highly sophisticated ways using neuroscience to help support the promotion of their product.

So, for those of us who are predisposed to being prisoners of the moment, there has simply been no more difficult time in which to live and be productive. This chapter took a look at the neuroscience of why and how we lose focus and what can be done to rewire the easily distractible brain. The intent is to deal with the source of what is causing the issue instead of simply providing solutions that only deal with the symptoms of the disease.

4

Checklist Dependent

Recently, I was sitting with a colleague in a regularly scheduled meeting for a community committee we served on together. We are old friends, so our meetings are less than formal, and she maintains an open-door policy. As we were meeting, a team leader came in to the office and looked flabbergasted. He asked if he could sit down and have a moment of her time. She looked at him a bit confused since I was clearly already sitting across from her at the desk. He then looked at me and commented that he didn't want this to wait and it was fine if I stayed if she trusted my ability to keep something confidential.

The team leader continued, without naming names, to discuss another team member who was refusing to move in the agreed-upon direction for the school. This staff member had a reputation of being a "conspiracy theorist" whenever any teacher had a strong relationship with administration; therefore, the team leader had little credibility or ability to move the initiative forward with the staff member in question.

Dr. Anthony Muhammad refers to these teachers as *fundamentalists* in his book *Transforming School Culture* (2010). Fundamentalists are educators who are comfortable with the status quo and subsequently work against any viable form of change. Their goal is to be left alone. They have many tools they use to thwart reform initiatives, and without the proper leadership, they are generally successful. The fundamentalist's personal needs and goals are paramount to the needs of students and the organization as a whole.

The team leader voiced his frustration and asked the principal (my colleague) for help. He sincerely believed that he didn't have the ability to push the action forward without her direct support. My colleague, normally relational and upbeat, appeared a bit glazed over. After a few moments, she thanked the team leader for his time and let him know that she would add it to her checklist of things to do. When she uttered those words, both parties looked defeated.

Once the team leader left, I jokingly asked how long her list had become. She said it was too long to recount and held up a legal pad with a sad but impressive list of tasks that needed to be completed. I had to ask, "How old is the oldest item on that list?"

She paused, looked down, and replied that it was at least 10 or 12 days old. We sat in silence for a few moments as she processed. "I guess it's not much a to-do list if the items on here aren't getting done," she remarked.

The intent of to-do lists is to organize work and provide focus for the task(s) at hand. In theory, to-do lists are exactly the type of solution you'd expect to find in a book about maximizing personal efficiency. The issue is that an overreliance on to-do lists and checklists serves to inhibit growth and does not maximize personal effectiveness. Moreover, to-do lists that are implemented incorrectly perpetuate ineffective traits instead of creating new and improved habits.

As always, there are two sides to every coin. If you are committed to to-do lists and find them extraordinarily efficient and effective, then this chapter might not apply to you. This chapter is for those who struggle to get everything done in a timely fashion and cause themselves undue stress while leveraging a to-do list or checklist as their survival tool.

Execution Is All That Matters

It is 5:00 a.m. and you arrive at the gym. Internally, you are congratulating yourself for getting out of bed and making it this far. The trainer starts in with his standard motivational quips: "The day is what you make it!" "Remember, you chose to be here!" "Whatever you don't give, right here in this moment, will be lost forever!"

You try and get into it, but it's just not there today. You turn up the music in your headphones in an attempt to drown out the motivational cries coming from a way-too-enthusiastic instructor. About 20 minutes into the 50-minute class, you start to do what you vowed you wouldn't do this year. You start watching the eyes of the instructor and taking reps off when he's not looking.

One thought races through your head: *Just. Get. Through. It.*

Even if you don't make a habit of going to the gym, we have all had that moment where we decide to just survive. To just get through something. This takes different forms for different people, but we've all been there. It might be making it through a sermon at church, faking it through a professional development session, or tolerating the time you've volunteered to a charity organization. When faced with that situation, we flip our mindsets to survival mode and simply comply with what is required of us in in the moment without expending any unnecessary physical or mental energy.

Here's the truth, though. Whenever your focus is simply to make it through something, you're not giving it 100 percent. As a result, you're not taking 100 percent away from it. We have the ability to choose to be curious, to be engaged, and to give max effort. That trainer in the gym? He's right. What you fail to give may as well be lost forever.

So what does this have to do with checklists and to-do lists? If you are an educator, everything. The reason is that very few tasks that need to be completed throughout the day are compliance oriented; instead, they require quick reactions and complex thought. Sure, you might need to remember to send a parent an email, which is simple enough. But a majority of tasks require critical thought, demonstrate the need to understand context, and evolve rapidly. Indeed, an educator makes more decisions on a daily basis than a brain surgeon. Everything is variable. Always.

While constructing a checklist for the day's activities is a decent starting point to organize your thoughts and drive action, it is simply not complex enough to move the needle on individual efficiency and effectiveness. Checking things off a to-do list provides a rush, to be sure, but it doesn't allow you to experience your day in a way that has the potential to make the biggest impact on those you serve.

The bottom line is that 41 percent of items placed on a to-do list never get completed (Kruze, 2015). Generally speaking, to-do lists and daily checklists simply do not work to drive action and effectiveness.

Signs You Are Checklist Dependent

Checklist-dependent people desire structure and order in their life. This is either an innate desire or an intentional decision to compensate for a potential area of growth. For those who experience time management issues, order and stability are incredibly attractive as attempts to regain control of your time (and, therefore, your life). People who are checklist dependent may care more about making a checklist and revisiting it several times a day rather than actually completing the tasks on the list. Similarly, they may search all week for the perfect app to support their to-do list but give no thought to some of the more complex tasks actually on the list. Checklist dependent people have a desire for order, stability, and efficiency—but a to-do list often is not the answer to their personal struggles with time and self-management.

You Spend More Time Making the Checklist
Than Working on the Tasks

An important distinction exists between those who use checklists effectively to manage time and those who do not. Those who use checklists well focus on charting a concrete path to improved results. The joy is not in creating the recipe but in cooking the meal.

The task at hand is not the creation of a document to guide the work of the day. The task is to complete the work of the day both efficiently and effectively. Nobody gets excited by printing out the directions for the drive to Disneyland; people get excited about arriving at Disneyland.

So, if you find yourself spending more time constructing a checklist or to-do list than you do in completing the work you're organizing, then you may be checklist dependent. Moreover, the checklist—which is ostensibly a tool for efficiency—is serving to slow your efforts down instead of speed them up.

You Enjoy the Rush of Checking Things Off

It is often said that the greatest competitors are not obsessed with winning; they are obsessed with *not* losing. Tennis great Jimmy Connors is famous for saying, "I hate losing more than I love to win." This type of attitude compels us to act and execute. Often, those who are checklist dependent (in an unhealthy way) get great pleasure from checking things off their to-do lists, but they gain no stress or drive for action by the items that remain on this list. This is the reason for the symptomatic performance or time management issue. When we like to accept the reward or affirmation of crossing an item off a checklist more than we are motivated to attack the incomplete items, then checklist dependency becomes an unhealthy habit.

If you are unsure if this is how you operate or not, take a minute and grab your to-do list. If you see an item that is more than three days old that isn't driving you crazy, you might be checklist dependent. If you see an item that is more than three days old and you aren't reprioritizing your day in order to get that work done, you might be checklist dependent.

If you behave in this manner, then your checklists are not used to keep track of what needs to get done. They have transformed into tools to keep track of what you have already gotten done.

You Abandon the List in the Face of Stress

I imagine there are still skeptics out there who are on the fence regarding the effectiveness of their checklist usage. One final self-check can help you determine if your checklist or to-do list is really doing anything to affect your productivity and efficiency.

When things really go sideways in a day, what do you do? We have all been there. A random email comes in the morning with a request to get something done ASAP or by EOB (dreaded acronyms!). As you figure out how you're going to fit it in, a colleague comes down with the stomach flu and the small amount of free time you had just vanished since you now have to cover some of her duties. If you had a stress meter, it would be dialed up to 11.

We all face stress and pressure in our personal and professional lives, but Weisinger (2015) makes a clear distinction between the two:

- **Stress** results from situations that have too many demands and not enough resources (e.g., time, money, energy) to meet them.
- **Pressure** results from situations in which you perceive that something is dependent on the outcome of your performance.

In moments such as these—during the craziest and most unpredictable days—are you more or less driven by your checklist? This is a telltale sign. Checklist-dependent people who do not use the tool as a true asset abandon their lists when the going gets tough. They allow unpredictable events to determine the course of their day. They have relatively little control. Events are happening to them, and they're just responding to those events. The question, then, is clear. What is the point of having the list in the first place?

Why You Love Checklists

Before we move on, it is important to understand that our desire to keep track of what we need to and what we've done is natural. It decreases anxiety and introduces structure—and yes, everyone loves the implicit reward of checking things off the list. Our love of to-do lists can be boiled down to three reasons: they dampen anxiety about the chaos of life; they provide a structure, a solid plan we can stick to; and they are proof of what we have achieved that day, week, or month (Chunn, 2017). Still, these benefits don't make them inherently successful at solving time management issues.

This chapter may seem like an assassination attempt on the institution of checklists and to-do lists. It certainly is not intended to be one. The issue here is a dependency on the tool to drive action and eliminate time management issues. It's all too clear that when lists are used as a remedy for a lack of efficiency or self-management, they often lead to failure. Consider this analogy. A checklist is to efficiency like a diet is to weight loss. The diet isn't the issue; it's our inability to use the diet effectively, consistently, and in times of stress that prevent it from creating the intended benefits.

Coping Mechanisms

Disaggregate your to-do list from email. If you are keeping your email as a to-do list, it is probably not working for you. I'm not going to try and convince you to be part of the 0-inbox club (which is an absolutely glorious club to be a part of) if that's not your style. However, I strongly suggest you take the time to establish your list elsewhere and not use your email inbox as a to-do list.

Here are a few quick reasons why this does not work:

- The list will just grow (and grow, and grow, and grow).
- There is no sense of urgency to remove something from a list with hundreds or thousands (you know who you are) of messages already within it.
- One part of your life does not become more organized by creating more clutter in a different part.

This is how you do it simply. For those of you who like to keep your inbox as a to-do list or are accustomed to organizing your life electronically, I could make an extensive list of apps that are all designed to do the same thing: help you manage your life and clean out your inbox. Since the life of these apps is so volatile, I will instead focus on two that have demonstrated their staying power and have significant benefits for the checklist-dependent reader: Todoist and Google Keep.

Todoist has been around for more than a decade. This may not seem old, but in today's add-on and app environment, it may as well be dog years. Todoist has over 10 million registered users and is continuing to grow. It does the same thing that many other apps in this category do. Namely, it helps to organize and prioritize your life by giving users access to create an electronic to-do list that is essentially always available—considering it is stored in a smartphone app. Todoist earns recognition in this book, however, because of the company's ethos. They are committed to helping people maximize their life in the same manner I am. Therefore, I believe (and hope) they will stick around for the long haul, so when someone picks this book up several years down the road, it will still be a worthy recommendation.

Google Keep is far and away the favorite app of this type in my current district. Google Keep launched in 2013 to mixed reviews, but it has continued to add options and features and is now a fan favorite. Google Keep is an all-encompassing note-taking app that consolidates information gathered in a variety of ways to assist in optimum organization. Although it's not specifically designed for time management and to-do lists, the app's functionality allows for it to be more than adequate in this capacity. The best benefit (as voiced by my staff) is the easy link to other Google apps and add-ons and its ability to leverage voice.

Use a commitment device. An overall lack of commitment devices inhibits the success of many to-do lists. Simply put, writing something down does not make you choose a less desirable task that may be more important. The term *commitment device* sounds somewhat formal, but it is intended to help articulate a position that we sometimes need artificial and arbitrary mechanisms to help focus our work.

Do you remember the example I used in Chapter 3 when I had to surrender my cell phone as a form of self-moderation? To-do lists don't prevent you from choosing the most pleasant tasks over the most important (and often most difficult) ones because they lack commitment devices that lock you into a course of action you might not otherwise choose.

This is not a new concept. The Chinese general Han Xin used geography as a commitment device. He positioned his soldiers with their backs to a river so they couldn't run away from the enemy (Markovitz, 2012). We do it when we diet by throwing out high-calorie and unhealthy foods. There is also a way to do it, though much less dramatically, to eliminate distractions and improve our productivity and commitment to to-do lists.

For instance, there is software that disables your internet access for a predetermined period of time. This is a commitment device. Some people use accountability partners. Take my device, and I will take yours; let's grind out this important task for the next few hours. This is a commitment device. Some people delete social media apps from their phone when they arrive at work. This is a commitment device. The point is that there are many different kinds of commitment devices, but they all have the same purpose. They all help us commit deeply to the work we have assigned ourselves through the to-do list process.

Reduce to seven. Humans thrive on options. It is wonderful to have choices in everything we do, from the jobs we pursue in our careers to what we eat for lunch. However, there is such a thing as too much of a good thing. Often, when we create lists, the sheer amount of work to be completed can be overwhelming and seem impossible. The challenge of picking where to begin sometimes results in analysis paralysis.

Iyengar and Lepper (2000) have shown that the human brain maxes out at seven options before we're overwhelmed. It is easier for us to make decisions—and we tend to make better decisions—when there are fewer choices from which to choose. The most likely reaction to seeing 83 items on a to-do list is to avoid all of them and check Facebook instead.

Solutions

Understand the Dopamine Rush

The brain is an amazing thing. Simply going through the process of writing a to-do list often makes us feel better, which actually has a demonstrated cognitive effect on our brains (Masicampo & Baumeister, 2011). Put another way, the simple act of making a plan can free you from anxiety and make you feel more effective. However, you need to keep in mind that it does not inherently make you more effective or a better manager of your own time.

When a to-do list includes relatively simple tasks, such as returning a library book, along with more complex tasks, such as writing a weekly newsletter, our brains are wired to focus on the shorter one. Why? Dopamine! The psychological payoff and dopamine release that comes from crossing an item off your list is awesome, which makes sense when you know that dopamine is a feel-good neurotransmitter associated with euphoria (and addiction). The desire to continue to complete tasks drives us toward the easier and shorter tasks and means some of those tasks—such as proofreading 75 pages of the new curriculum guide—will wait a long, long time.

Thus, understanding that the brain's natural tendency to seek out easier tasks to complete and reward itself with a dopamine rush is essential to creating lasting personal change. As is the focus throughout this book, true change happens from within, and a deeper understanding of our brain and the way we think and react can help us create lasting personal change. With this understanding in mind, it becomes easier to create and be mindful of the to-do lists we make and manage.

Make If-Then Lists

The best to-do lists are thoughtfully constructed. That means that if you are going to spend five minutes every morning organizing your tasks, then it's better to spend 10 minutes and organize them in a way that truly increases your efficiency and effectiveness.

One simple technique to do this is the if-then to-do list. And, yes, they are as easy to use as they seem.

If/When I _____, I will work on _____.

Consider the following examples;

- When 4 p.m. rolls around, I will drop everything and make phone calls home to parents.
- When I finish writing the assessment, I will work on scripting questions for tomorrow's lesson.
- If I have no emergencies this morning, I will work on my report for the Board of Education.

- If I get distracted, I will drop everything at 10 a.m. and dedicate an hour to writing my report.

This simple adjustment works for multiple reasons. First, it forces prioritization during the day as opposed to simply constructing a list of activities. Second, it inherently provides an accountability partner in you. The act of writing tasks in this manner—rather than jotting down tasks to be done in no particular order—triggers you to hold yourself more accountable to your word.

Determine Complexity, Timeliness, and Importance

Here is the crux of the issue with checklists. We tend to conflate variable tasks and count them all as equal. Item #1 on the list may be to call back a parent, and item #2 may be to construct a unit plan for the Civil War. One takes 10 minutes; the other may take 10 hours. Nevertheless, on the average to-do list, they appear equal. And somewhere in the recesses of our minds, we have trained ourselves to be happy if there are only one or two items left on the to-do list.

As a result of this mentality, we focus more on the reward of crossing something off the list than we do on what is going to help us accomplish our goals as professionals. That being said, the items that are often left to fester are the complex items requiring time, effort, energy, and critical thought.

If you believe you need a checklist or to-do list in order to maximize effectiveness, simply add a few columns. A template is provided in Figure 4.1, but there are many different ways to improve the typical to-do list.

These simple additions allow you to map out your day instead of choosing to complete random tasks (which ends up like picking the low-hanging fruit). We have the choice each day whether we want to do the important work necessary to provide the experience our kids and adults deserve. A modified to-do list serves to help you attack the day.

Figure 4.1

Checklist Template

To Do	Time for Expected Completion	Level of Thought/ Focus Needed	Priority Level (High, Medium, Low)

Create Lists That Match Your Priorities

The bottom line is that what we value is what gets done. If you are struggling with staying on top of tasks at work (or at home), and it is apparent that your peers are not having the same struggles, then the issue may be in what you value. If everyone else can execute at a different level in the 8–12 hours they spend at work each day and you cannot, I am willing to bet your to-do list doesn't match your priorities.

To say it another way, the problem isn't your talent or capacity. You are most likely talented beyond belief and can accomplish great things. The issue, then, is your willingness to commit to the work that needs to be done because it does not match what you like to do or what you value doing.

When I work with educators, I frequently see the checklist item that receives the least attention is the person who made the list. That means you. This is why self-care is so important. Getting to the gym, taking time to meditate, and premaking meals to stay on your diet are all, in essence, pretty simple tasks. The trouble is that we allow other stuff to get in the way of doing the important things for ourselves. Simply put, you cannot take care of everyone else if you do not take care of yourself. Live your life based on priorities—not just empty action. And make sure *you* are resoundingly one of your own priorities.

Final Thoughts

Checklists are an effective way of reducing variability when completing procedures of varying complexity. They are great at documenting transferable good practice but are not a great way to self-monitor and drive our work. Life is too complex and complicated to be driven by an arbitrary list of items jotted down on a piece of paper.

Throughout this chapter, I've exposed some errors in thinking that drive our to-do list culture. If you love to-do lists, there are ways of making them so much more effective than sticky notes scrambled all over your desk or a half-ripped piece of paper with items only you can figure out scribbled upon them.

Checklists and to-do lists can serve a great function. However, if you feel as though your to-do lists are constantly growing—and you are not becoming more effective and efficient—then it is time to take a hard look at your own practice and adapt.

5

Disorganized

My middle son, Jackson, is a great kid. He's always smiling and is naturally kind. He's the kind of child who floats through life as if he doesn't have a care in the world. I often think that he would be more appropriately positioned somewhere on a beach with flip-flops instead of suffering through winters in Illinois.

While I envy his laid-back attitude (I can be wound a little tight), his lack of concern for most everything also spills over into his lack of concern for organization and schoolwork. Let's face it, all kids can struggle from time to time with organization, but Jackson takes it to a different level. As a 5th grader, he had to ask us to sign a field trip permission slip four times. We would sign it—even supervise him placing it in the appropriate folder— and then a few days later, we would be asked again. This routine continued over the course of two weeks. His inability to organize his life, even with assistance, was astounding.

Whenever I attempt to teach organizational skills, the situation temporarily improves, but two weeks later we're back to the same disorganized mess when it comes to his backpack, folders, and locker. Then he hits me with "But Dad, I heard that messy people are smarter. Is that true?" I admit that Einstein was famously messy and often incredibly creative people have a hard time keeping mundane things in order.

I remind him that messy should not be his goal and then ask if he likes being messy or if it just makes his life harder in the long run. He notes that he hates being disorganized when it costs him time and effort. Being organized just isn't important to him until it comes back to bite him when he cannot find something or has to redo it.

The lessons to be learned from this are plentiful. The badge of honor that many wear for being disorganized is, in the vast majority of cases, simply a tool to deflect internal and external criticism for their lack of organization. What does that mean? It means that a significant majority of people who are disorganized are negatively affecting not only their own productivity through their sloppiness but also their mental well-being by not taking steps to address a perpetual problem.

Depend On or Be Depended On

In my experience, there are two types of people in this world. This holds true for friends, colleagues, bosses, employees, spouses, and family. You either need to depend on other people or you can be depended on. For me, there are few compliments that mean more than a colleague, friend, or family member telling me they could always count on me. This type of mutual accountability and service to each other is unmatched, and it cannot be faked.

It is absolutely true that we all need to depend on others throughout our lives, but I trust that you are able to think of at least one person on whom you know you can always count. Likewise, I'm sure you can also think of at least one person who always depends on others, even to his or her detriment. I encourage you to think about this in the context of work. Is there one person who always has the assignment, memo, or policy handy? Is there one person who routinely sends out an email begging for help? In many instances, this is a binary truth; either others count on you or you count on others.

There are no universals, but disorganized people seem to be disproportionately likely to depend on others to get the job done. Efficiency and effectiveness wanes when time, effort, and energy are spent trying to find something that could easily be at your fingertips. This type of routine self-imposed distraction is exactly the type of thing that leads people to be managed by their time instead of driving their daily work on their own terms.

Signs You Are Disorganized

Some disorganized people may not feel the need for order in their life. An attempt to become more organized is predicated on an understanding that disorganization is having a negative effect on someone's timeliness and work production. However, when that moment of incredible self-awareness kicks in, it becomes an attractive premise to attempt to regain control of your time (and therefore your life) through personal reorganization.

You Cannot Find Important Information

We have all had a flash of momentary panic when we cannot find an important form that needs a signature or an email we knew we needed to keep. In addition, we've all had that moment when we put something important in a place we would never forget—only to forget about it 18 hours later. This latter scenario is 100 percent me with my driver's license or passport every time I get ready to travel, which inevitably leads to 30 seconds of sheer and epic panic (sometimes in the airport security line).

My point is we can all relate to that feeling. The real issue is *how often* you relate to that feeling. If reading the previous paragraph made you flash back to one instance that happened eight months ago and another from just over a year ago, rest easy. This is not a sign that you are disorganized. However, if you relate to these examples and something similar happens so often that the panic-induced adrenaline rush that occurs when you cannot find something no longer floods your system, then that *is* a sign you may be disorganized.

You Rely on Others More than They Rely on You

There are two types of people in every work environment: the type that people go to for help and the type that are always asking for help. This does not refer to new team members who are learning the ropes and finding their way; rather, this refers to people who are grounded and well established in their roles. Nobody starts a new job with the intention of performing beneath expectations so that colleagues and coworkers can't trust their ability to follow through. Still, this occurs.

There is a simple self-test to see if this applies to you. Think back over the last month of work. Who has asked you for help, advice, or a key document? By contrast, how many times have you had to ask for help, advice, or a key document that you should have already had in your possession?

To be clear, this may or may not have anything to do with the quality of your work. It is entirely possible that you are completely disorganized and unreliable, but when you complete work, it is done at an incredible level. Remember, the context of this book is how to increase efficiency and effectiveness on the job—not to condemn the work that is being completed. Some disorganized people are the smartest and most effective workers I know; the issue is they are not maximizing their impact due to a lack of organization.

People Avoid Your Personal Space

If you have (or have had at some point) tween or teenage kids, this will make perfect sense. Remember the sense of dread you felt when giving someone a tour of the house or pointing them to the upstairs bathroom knowing they may see the bathroom or bedroom of your adorable little angel(s)? Well, this may be happening to you in the office. It may be subtle or it may be overt, but it is most likely happening if your personal space is a mess.

Moreover, *you* may be the one making this decision based on your personal space. I have colleagues who never want to meet with parents in their classroom because of the apparent disorganization on their desk. Similarly, some of my principals vastly prefer to use a conference room rather than their office because their disorganization is embarrassing and not representative of the professional they aspire to be.

Still not sure if this describes you? Think about your car and which vehicle is used when your friends or colleagues need to carpool. If your car (and your driving) is on par with those of your peers, but nobody ever wants to ride with you, then that may be a clue that your disorganization has been noticed and is reflected in your relationships with friends and coworkers. Simply put, nobody wants to ride in a horribly messy car, particularly when an alternative exists.

People Keep Sending You Reminders

I hate sending email, memos, or voicemails that reference some form of previous communication and then restate an expectation or request (e.g., per our last email . . .). They are not fun to send and even less fun to receive. However, for some people, they are neither pleasant nor alarming; they're just the norm. If you feel that way when you receive such communication from a parent, colleague, or supervisor, then you most likely suffer from significant disorganization.

To explain, we typically become desensitized to something after we've been exposed to it multiple times. For instance, a coach who always yells at her players gets no immediate change in behavior by simply yelling. But the mild-mannered and calm coach who infrequently raises her voice will undoubtedly get the attention of her team when she starts yelling.

If the reminder of your personal inability to respond to a request does not startle you, then there is a good chance you are disorganized and have grown somewhat immune to what *should* be an alarming reminder. There is always a possibility that these reminders do not create a sense of urgency or concern for another reason, such as your opinion of the person making the request or your confidence in your ability to finish on time; however, disorganization is certainly likely to be the root cause of this issue.

Coping Mechanisms

Reduce paper. Reducing the amount of paper in your life might seem like a good starting point on the road to organization (and it is!), but you have to be careful. It is also possible to be disorganized electronically. The good news is that it's just a little less likely, and there are more fail-safes in a life that is organized electronically.

For the skeptic who recognizes the advantages of electronic organization but doesn't know what to do with the pile(s) of paperwork currently on desks and crammed into drawers, there are a variety of answers. First and foremost, the simple act of going through those stacks is healthy. Almost universally, there will be paperwork taking up your workspace from a lesson completed months ago or from a professional development activity that is so old you cannot even remember the speaker. It's okay to process these materials and move on.

I know what you're thinking. This definitely sounds time-intensive. The reality of the situation is that getting organized *is* time-intensive. In fact, going from disorganized to organized unequivocally takes longer than just doing something right the first time. We all know this. We say it constantly to our students and children. The mountain of work you have sitting in front of

you is real, but so are the problems and inefficiencies it is causing right now.

These four easy steps can be taken today to help you reduce
paper and start to get more organized.

- **Make three piles.** They should include papers that are (1)
  important enough to keep but not to file, (2) important
  enough to keep and must keep on file, and (3) not important
  enough to keep. This system may seem simple, but to someone who suffers from disorganization, the simple classification system helps immensely. It is often the first step that is
  hardest to take, so by creating three piles, the first step is
  taken for you.
- **Use files or binders.** There should never be paper just hanging
  out, free. If it is important enough to keep, then it is important
  enough to file or place in a binder with other key information.
  There is nothing that exists on paper that does not deserve
  enough attention to file or place in an organizing binder.
- **Recognize that the scanner is your friend.** Almost all copi-
  ers have built-in scanners and the ability to email. If this
  level of technology is not available at your school, you can
  also use your phone as a scanner. Simply take a picture and
  use one of a variety of apps to turn that photo into a PDF
  document. I am not exaggerating when I say that there are
  easily 20 ways to do this for free. A quick search of the iOS
  or Android app stores will turn up a bunch of options.
- **Remember that digital is nothing without folders.** My
  biggest fear in providing these suggestions is that they will
  only create a digitally disorganized person. Folders are necessary to keep your life organized digitally. Here's a quick
  check: if you have Word, Excel, PowerPoint, or PDF files
  saved directly on your desktop or documents tab—and not
  organized into clearly named folders—you need to get yourself organized. There is no pride in having a clean desk and
  a horribly disorganized desktop.

Force a relocation. Drastic times call for drastic measures. Sometimes the only way people can force themselves to get organized and purge unnecessary materials is to relocate. This may be as dramatic as asking your supervisor for a change in classrooms or as simple as moving your desk from the back to the front of the classroom or from one side of the office to the other.

The point is that nobody moves a dirty desk. Also, nobody wants to move a heavy desk. This seems simple—and it is, particularly if you follow the advice on how to reduce paper. There is a theme here that is necessary to understand. If you are disorganized, the overwhelming likelihood is that you have *too much stuff*. Remember, if everything is important, then nothing is important. Simply put, geography matters and can make a difference. Take the drastic step of moving your stuff, even if it's only a few feet. The change forces you (at least momentarily) to face the negative behavior head-on and work toward a solution.

Mitigate the impact of your disorganization. There are some of you reading this right now who may identify with being disorganized. You may even be convinced that disorganization is hindering your efficiency at work and thereby affecting your life. Despite that recognition, these coping mechanisms might still feel like monumental tasks to take on that you just don't have time for at the moment. I get that.

If that's the case, then this coping mechanism is precisely for you. If disorganization is something with which you struggle, but you are unwilling to invest the time and effort required to rid yourself of this negative habit, then I implore you to at least work to mitigate the impact this trait is having on your performance.

Chronic disorganization can be mitigated in three simple ways, which can be employed together or independently.

- **Create a sacred space.** As disorganized as someone may be, it's still possible to create a sacred space for important materials they know they will have to revisit. This space can be a corner of a desk, a file folder, a desk organizer—literally anything. If you tend to keep everything and do not want to address the larger issue surrounding that habit, then you can expend a smaller amount of mental energy to presort materials. This way, when you are panicked and looking for something specific, you won't need to frantically search your entire office, backpack, and backseat of your car. Instead, you'll just need to check one spot designated for this purpose.

- **Phone a friend.** When we look at possible solutions, we will discuss this issue in greater detail, but some people genuinely struggle to understand what is important and what might be revisited in the future. The simple technique of asking a trusted friend or colleague (you know, that one person everyone depends on) whether this is something that needs to be earmarked for future use is a huge step in addressing this issue. It will not only provide you with quick, real-time feedback on a singular issue that needs addressing but also demonstrate vulnerability and the willingness to grow to your colleagues.

  To elaborate, when you leave a meeting and have seven different pieces of paper in your hand that were all explained as important, pull Mary or Joe or Elaine to the side. Ask them which documents they believe you should keep handy and which ones you can file away. One issue that many disorganized people face is an inability to make decisions when it comes to what is important. This process eliminates that decision.

- **Color-code or flag your documents.** Another option is to invest in some color paper. The strategy is simple: copy important documents on appropriately color-coded paper. For instance, items pertaining to curriculum are yellow and actionable documents from your boss are blue. This way, if your disorganized ways continue, at least there is a "decoder ring" in place to help you find your way out of the mess you created.

This can also be done electronically in several ways. Instead of color coding, you can use naming and sorting techniques. We have already discussed a folder system, but using naming strategies also works for many people. My father, for instance, demonstrates the value of a document by placing an AA in front of it. When he sorts his documents alphabetically, the most important documents come to the top. Once a document has lost its relevancy, the title remains the same, but the AA prefix is deleted.

Solutions

Understand the Real Issue

Messiness is not laziness. Messiness is also not a sign of genius. It's not that incredibly smart people cannot also be messy. Sure, it can be a sign of creativity, but more often than not it is indicative of something completely different. Messiness and disorganization are difficult constructs to grasp.

Psychiatrist Marcia Sirota (2010) believes she has a construct that explains messiness. Disorganized people tend to become overwhelmed by "stuff," get lost in the problem, and quit attempting to solve it. As a result, disorganized people find themselves in a literal and figurative mess. The solution is to help make their lives more manageable by "chunking" their stuff.

The solution is in grasping that no person is born inherently messy. Though some people may prefer perfect order and others have a more relaxed approach, nobody chooses to be disorganized to the extent that their lives become more difficult and they become less effective and efficient as a result. By working to deeply understand that messiness (unless spurred on by a true psychological disorder and diagnosis) is a result of underdeveloped organizational skills—more than it is a decision not to care—any educator can make strides to create lasting personal change.

It is important to realize that even the most organized person in education can be overwhelmed by the sheer amount of stuff flying at them. New initiatives, papers to grade, social media notifications, and "real life" very quickly combine to form a flood of information. It is vital to understand that messiness is not a disease; it is essentially a large self-directed (albeit often unintentional) coping mechanism to deal with the madness of life.

Strategize for the Long Term

Everything in life takes time. People who struggle to be efficient and manage their time effectively often try to find ways to maximize the time they do have. In doing so, they make the incorrect decision of forgoing organization for what appears—at first glance—to be efficiency. The issue is, disorganization costs us far more time in the long run than it saves us in the short term.

With that in mind, keep in mind that time spent up front saves you time on the back end. For those of you who simply cannot operate in this fashion, then you need to schedule time to clean up the mini-messes you are creating through lack of organization before they become macro-messes. Take 15 minutes at the start of every Monday and Wednesday and 5 minutes at the end of every Friday and dedicate it to organizing your world. It will save you time, effort, and energy in the future. I guarantee it.

It might not be intuitive to think that spending time doing something new and different in addition to everything you are already doing will help with time management, but if it were intuitive, then everybody would already be doing it. For the vast majority of the human population, living in an orderly environment is psychologically and emotionally beneficial. Neuroscientist Kelly Clancy (2014) explores the concept that our brain is always working between order and chaos and seeks out both. The more order we provide to the environment in which we live, the more brain power we have to use on the tasks that fill up our increasingly unpredictable days.

Develop an Information Triumvirate

In the Coping Mechanisms section of this chapter, you were presented with a sorting system to help get your life organized. A similar sorting mechanism is shared here, but this moves beyond the simplicity of trying to get organized at a single point in time. This system is one that can sustain and be used to guide your thinking as you build a new habit that supports your organizational skills.

There are three types of information, documents, and artifacts that need to be kept.

- **Information you need to refer to regularly.** I like to call these *resources*. They are nonactionable items that need to be accessed quickly and will likely stay relevant for an extended period of time.
- **Information that needs to be passed on to someone else.** This information does not stop with you. For teachers, this may be a lesson planning template that needs to be returned to a supervisor or an essay that needs to get back to a student. They are items of temporary ownership.
- **Information that you will need to return to at a specific point in time.** This is something that may be complete but needs to be revisited down the road. For instance, it might be a report on student data that needs to be referenced after the next benchmark.

Deliberate practice is the only way to gain effectiveness and expertise in any facet of life. This is even more important in areas where you may not be naturally talented. As a result, this simple three-tier classification system presents a template or model to use as you continue down a path of increasing your personal effectiveness. Is this framework all-encompassing and a perfect representation of everything that will come your way as an educator? No, but nothing in life is perfect. This is a framework that helps you continue to react and respond to the radically unpredictable and ever-changing world of education.

Final Thoughts

Being organized is a skill that can be practiced. It takes intentional thought and effort, in addition to patience and time. For those of you who read this chapter and found that it resonated with you, remember that the issue is not that you are lazy. Erase that negative self-talk from your mind. The issue is that you do not currently have the mindset and/or skills to attack each day in a manner that allows you to stay organized and productive. A shift in your actions will ultimately lead to a shift in your outcomes.

6

Technology Avoidant

I learned everything I know about work from my father. That may seem odd, considering my father never attended a day of higher education and couldn't tell you the difference between curriculum and corduroy. My dad started as a janitor and worked his way up to middle management in a steel fabrication factory. He personifies rugged Midwestern values and is a lot tougher than I will ever be. He drove a broken-down Oldsmobile Cutlass over an hour round-trip to work every single day. A car I would hate driving today never seemed to bother him.

My dad would often work 16-hour days so he could earn overtime money and help us move from a less desirable neighborhood into an area renowned for high-quality schools. He would even leave work to coach my Little League games and then immediately go back—turning his 16-hour workday into a 19-hour workday.

He is the epitome of someone achieving the American dream, and he's a wonderful father. My dad is someone who willed and worked his way through life to give his family a better chance at success than he had. He was also *very* short on words, so I learned these lessons through observation—not through him trying to overtly teach me.

In short, my dad was tough and *never* complained.

Until one day when I was around 16 years old. One evening, he came home and was in a bad mood. This was not completely abnormal, but opening up and complaining about it at the dinner table certainly was. He had a new boss who was adamant about him starting to use email. Yes, email. By this point in my father's career, he was in middle management, but any skills he had on the computer, in leadership, or in organization were self-taught. This new wrinkle was not something my father wanted to learn in his 50s. He saw email as completely unnecessary.

He rebelled. He tried to stand firm. In the end, of course, he gave in. My father bet against email, and email won. Resoundingly. A lot of people have done this or something similar. Indeed, a lot of people are still doing this, just in different ways. Think of all the social media doubters who still exist. Heck, even I would have bet against Snapchat in 2015.

Now think of all of the roadblocks we put up in our schools to eliminate social media use instead of teaching kids how to use it appropriately. By not allowing our kids to access the very tool that defines their generation, we implicitly give our faculty and staff permission to not embrace or learn about this culture-changing movement.

Let me shine a little light on technology for anyone who is reading this and cringing. Facebook's valuation is currently over $500 billion. Social media is not going anywhere. Technology is not going anywhere. And change is going to continue to happen at an ever-increasing rate. Twenty-five years ago, Netflix, Amazon, and Google didn't exist, and we have no idea what technological advancements will affect us 25 years from now. The question becomes whether we are going to leverage those tools to help us become better and more efficient at what we do, or are we going to ignore the single most revolutionary development of our lives the way my dad tried to ignore email?

We still have educators who refuse to embrace technology, or they embrace it in a very limited fashion. The Consortium for School Networking (2008) notes that in a study of large professional fields, education ranked last in terms of technology integration—even behind coal mining! Despite this, it is possible to be incredibly effective at your job and still be technology avoidant. Great teachers and educators will never be replaced by technology. However, they could be replaced by other great educators who choose to use the most advanced and effective tools at their disposal.

That leaves us with a very simple choice. Any of us can choose to be technology avoidant, but why in the world would you want to work that much harder than everyone else to get the same results?

Fear

Technology-avoidant people are usually either fearful or stubborn. A fear of technology is not new, though. When the personal computer first became ubiquitous in the 1980s, some people found it so terrifying that the term *computerphobia* was coined (LaFrance, 2015). "Humans often converge around massive technological shifts—around any change, really—with a flurry of anxieties. In the early days of the telephone, people wondered if the machines might be used to communicate with the dead. Today, it is the smartphone that has people jittery" (para. 2).

The fear is normal, though not rational. In most cases, people have adjusted to the concerns that create this fear and have decided to use the technology to their advantage. Nevertheless, the fear remains for many people since they can't get past their lack of control. To explain, we will never have total control over the technology that makes a smartphone so amazing.

Acknowledging that it is impossible to control is, admittedly, unnerving and makes some people unwilling to commit to that technology to the point where it becomes a necessary part of their lives.

If this is you, know that you are not abnormal. In an annual study conducted at Chapman University (2015), more than 1,500 subjects (typically) are asked to rank things that caused them fear. Technology, and particularly technology that individuals do not personally understand, places alarmingly high. In some cases, it's as high as second place (behind natural disasters) and more than 30 places ahead of death! All that is to say, being technology avoidant does not make you the anomaly you may think, and this chapter is dedicated to providing you with some strategies for moving past your anxiety.

Signs You Are Technology Avoidant

This section of each chapter is designed to shine a light on behaviors that indicate the true problem behind the time management symptoms. This is much less necessary in this chapter. Everyone knows someone who is not proficient in technology. We know it; they know it. However, what if *you* are technology avoidant? Can you recognize it in yourself? This manifests itself in a myriad of ways including, but not limited to, keeping a paper calendar, printing out documents sent to you electronically, and embracing others who use technology—but refusing to do so yourself.

You Have a Paper Calendar

I am going to right to the heart of the matter. If you have a paper calendar, you are missing out on one of the best parts of the technologically superior world we have the privilege of living in. I've heard all the common excuses, and they're all false. Believe me.

Do you keep one family calendar because you think it is easier to have it in a centrally located place where anyone can adjust it? Think again. You can easily share a digital calendar across a plethora of platforms and give everyone real-time access from any computer or smartphone.

Do you think a paper calendar is the best way to stay organized and ensure that nothing is missed? Well, even if this is your truth, it runs counter to the thesis of this book in terms of maximizing your time and efficiency. I know many people reading this are probably bristling right now, and that is fine. I challenge you to critically think through your reasons why having a paper calendar is necessary. Is it really the most efficient use of your most finite resource: time?

I cannot make this simpler. Smartphone apps and the advancement of calendar platforms (primarily via Google and Outlook) have become unbeatable. In terms of time management, efficiency, and structure, there is nothing we can create on paper that compares to the advantages a digital calendar provides.

You Print Most Documents

Full disclosure: I still print some documents. I print anything I want to annotate or that I know I need to read closely to examine facts and figures. That doesn't mean I print *everything*. If your first instinct whenever you receive an email or attachment is to print, then you may well be technology avoidant.

In fact, many organizations have a disclaimer on their emails encouraging people not to simply print it out. They encourage people to think about the environment before hitting print on every email they may consider important.

This is a telltale sign, however, to determine if your use of the printer demonstrates that you are behind the times or technology avoidant. If you print things only to file them, you are technology avoidant. The same filing structure you are using in the tactile world is also available digitally, and it takes one less step! If you don't trust your computer and are afraid it may crash, or if the cloud fundamentally scares you, then check the box—you are technology avoidant and not maximizing your time.

You Are Less Hesitant Toward Technology When You Personally Benefit from It

If your child, mother, or significant other had a life-threatening health situation, would you want his or her doctors to use every tool at their disposal? The answer, no doubt, is an unequivocal *yes*. I for one would want the doctors to teleconference with the world's best specialists. I would fly my loved one to the operating room with the most advanced surgical techniques. I would pay any amount of money to have the lab specimens analyzed by the finest computers and shared across a complex network to have hundreds of experts analyze the results.

This makes me, most likely, no different from any of you.

The disconnect comes when we recognize that something is powerful and effective enough to warrant its use in times of personal crisis (or when you personally benefit from it), but we still refuse to embrace the same things on a daily basis. Technology has given us, and therefore our students, the ability to access expert-level information, connect with peers and thought leaders well beyond our ZIP code, and lead our own learning. If you realize all of this is out there and would want it used to your benefit on your behalf—but do not want to leverage it in your own practice—you now know you are technology avoidant.

Coping Mechanisms

Create nonnegotiables for yourself. One of the easiest ways to begin to address technology avoidance and attack resulting time management issues is to work with colleagues and establish some nonnegotiable requirements for your own behavior.

Accountability partners work in a variety of ways. One way is simply to agree to a certain course of action and come up with a compact of sorts. For the technology-avoidant person seeking to increase his or her time management skills, the following could be a great list of nonnegotiable behaviors (that should be revisited quarterly):

- Only print emails and/or attachments that are over three pages long.
- Begin entering events *only* in an electronic calendar.
- Save all documents to some type of cloud-supported platform (e.g., Google Drive, Dropbox, Sugarsync).
- Create at least one professional social media account.
- Self-select one app per month to explore at a self-directed pace.

Not only are these eminently doable tasks, they should also help fight the technology avoidant war on two fronts. First, they expose and create technology usage in a variety of manners. Each step is simple on its own and builds different skills. Second, and more directly to the purpose of this book, they help with time management and workplace efficiency.

Be strategic and gradual in your adoption. For those of us who love technology, one of the greatest features of the internet is that it is seemingly limitless. It is literally impossible to know every new app, development, trick, and technique that is created with education and time management in mind. The abundance of opportunities afforded by the internet can be liberating for some, but it can also be constricting. Humans frequently become paralyzed by choice, which is a problem most technology-avoidant people experience.

This is why intentional and scheduled practice is important for struggling technology adopters. Given that the primary focus of this book is how to self-diagnose and then remedy what ails us in the realm of time management, it would therefore be prudent to examine one preassigned app per month. Small, scheduled, and sustained successes have the ability to create momentum, increase efficiency, and (over time) change beliefs.

An example six-month calendar could be a simple as this:

- January: Find and utilize a calendar app.
- February: Find and utilize a social media platform.
- March: Find and utilize a to-do list feature on your email platform.
- April: Find and utilize a delayed-delivery feature within your email.
- May: Ask your best friend for one app he/she uses to be more effective and utilize it.
- June: Ask your professional network for one app they use to support time efficiency and utilize it.

Abandon the "pencil problem" myth. This is a technique that tends to flip the mindset (albeit temporarily) for many technology-avoidant educators. The simple question of what happens when a pencil breaks seems to have a profound impact on thinking. When, not if, a pencil breaks, we have two options. We either sharpen or repair the pencil or move on to some other type of writing utensil. In short, we find another way to get the job done, and we certainly do not blame the pencil or the concept of writing on paper.

This helps shift the practitioner away from focusing on the fallibility of technology. Technology is not perfect. Networks drop. Apps crash. People forget to save important documents. Viruses attack. Conversely, papers tear, dogs eat homework, and backpacks get stolen. The world is an imperfect place.

Change happens for people when they stop looking for excuses to fit their preconceived narrative. When people stop being technology avoidant, they look for problems that technology can help solve and deal with the minor inconveniences along the way. These are the same types of inconveniences we have ignored for decades when it comes to pencils, pens, paper, and backpacks. Either you accept small failures and keep your eye on the big picture, or you are consumed with the small failures and refuse to see the big picture.

Remember that it is not "one more thing." Technology-avoidant people typically see technology as one more thing to learn or do in a world where their plates continue to get fuller. This allows them to look at technology as a solution in search of a problem. This is an important conceptual understanding for both technology advocates and avoiders to wrestle with. There were great teachers before technology and there are great teachers because of technology. Both statements can be true and not make the other false. The question to ponder is whether an educator can be totally awesome in 2028 without significant technology usage. If this answer is *no*, then we must move forward today with that understanding in mind.

Once people on both sides of the fence (tech advocates and avoiders) realize that technology is not an initiative or a program, then the conversation becomes different—and simpler. Technology is a tool that helps us work toward our instructional goals and ultimately supports instruction. That's all there is to it.

If you have found yourself avoiding technology because it is one more thing in a never-ending list of add-ons, it's time to work on changing that perspective. You deserve it. You deserve something you can utilize to make your time more efficient and effective in all aspects of your job. Moreover, the students and communities you serve deserve to have someone who is using the very best tools of the day—just as we would demand the same of a doctor serving us.

Solutions

Admit the Value of Technology

One of the best steps someone who is technology avoidant can take is just admitting that technology and its role is very real and vitally important in our changing world. Sometimes, this admission is easier to make when supported by facts, such as those presented by best-selling author Erik Qualman (2017):

- Over 50 percent of the world's population is under 30 years old.
- Roughly 53 percent of millenials would rather lose their sense of smell than their technology.
- The return on investment of social media is that your business will still exist in five years.
- An astonishing 93 percent of buying decisions are influenced by social media.
- More people, worldwide, would rather own a mobile device than a toothbrush.
- One in three marriages start online.
- The fastest growing demographic on Twitter is grandparents.
- Every second, two people join LinkedIn.

It is here. It is real. It can be amazing. Come join the fun.

Invest in Your Growth

This may seem deceptively simple, but investing in personal growth and exposure is an amazing way to change the trajectory of your life. This is true in any scenario, but it's especially relevant when a fear of something is holding us back. If you claim that you do not have the time to learn technology—even though you know it will improve your work efficiency and effectiveness—then this section is for you.

Here are some simple, scientifically supported techniques to overcome fear: acknowledge, expose, manage, and practice.

- **Acknowledge.** We must first acknowledge that a fear or anxiety exists. That has been a core purpose and theme throughout this chapter. We cannot overcome something that we do not acknowledge exists. We must be vulnerable to and honest with ourselves in order to move forward to becoming the best version of ourselves (Livingstone, 2009).

- **Expose.** We must then expose ourselves to what we fear. We cannot get past something if we refuse to expose ourselves to it. The brain, when exposed to something it fears, goes through a process commonly referred to as fight or flight. This reaction starts in the amygdala, which is shaped like an almond and is located in the temporal lobe. The amygdala activates whenever we perceive or experience emotion. This reaction triggers the sympathetic nervous system and the release of stress hormones (Harvard Medical School, 2018). As the brain works through this process, it becomes much easier to give in to our fear and not put our body through this (quick) stressful process. Though it's inconvenient and uncomfortable, it is a crucial step to moving forward.

- **Manage.** Stress management is often easier said than done. Exercise and meditation are two of the most common strategies to eliminate stress. For those truly tech-phobic people out there who are committed to facing your fears, make sure you take care of yourself as you make the conscious decision to grow.

- **Practice.** Intentional and thoughtful practice aimed at conquering your fears will reduce stress (Gregoire, 2013). There is no way around this. The best medicine to stop being technology avoidant is to lean in to whatever concerns you have and work yourself past it. Be strategically gradual in your adoption to avoid getting overwhelmed. This is a great way to look your fear in the eye and start moving forward from technology avoidant to (perhaps, one day) technologically savvy.

When in doubt, remember this: you are not going to break the internet!

Find a Buddy

No great change happens overnight, and not much great change happens without someone helping along the way. You have a better chance of completing a goal if you publicly commit to someone else. And if you have a specific accountability appointment with a person to whom you've committed, you will increase your chance of success significantly. That is an absolutely mind-boggling statistic, but it all boils down to this: if you want to overcome being technology avoidant, you need to find someone to help you along the way.

Final Thoughts

Embracing a fear of technology is as simple as it is complex. The mental work necessary to get yourself from one end of the continuum to the other is enormous. The best part, however, is that a majority of that work is just that—mental. This is as much a competition within your own brain as it is a skill to be learned. It is easy to construct an argument about the complex nature of technological tools, but truly—you can do it! It is 100 percent about your mindset. All of us have the capacity to be successful at leveraging the tools of today.

7

Self-Server

Jennifer is great at her job. In fact, she is probably the best administrator that Dr. Morris has in his district. She is not the best employee, however. It is a very strange dichotomy. Jennifer has the ability to build relationships and cultivate trust, and she has formed an incredible culture in her school. The parents love her, the faculty loves her, and the students love her. And—for the most part—Dr. Morris loves her.

Right up until the point when he does not love her.

As great as Jennifer is within her building and with her staff, she is equally as divisive and demanding with the rest of the district team. Jennifer is notorious for bungling or mishandling paperwork and then causing a stir to ensure that her staff members get everything done appropriately. She has high expectations for others that she does not have for herself. As a result, everyone else's work appears to be deficient when the original problem was actually caused by Jennifer's lack of timeliness.

Jennifer is a disaster when it comes to timelines. If Dr. Morris needs something for a Thursday Board of Education meeting, he receives it late on Tuesday night and is asked to make an exception. If the monthly report to the district office is due on the 1st of the month, Jennifer's *may* trickle in somewhere around the 5th.

Dr. Morris is not afraid of holding his principals accountable. He has tried everything he can with Jennifer. Formal discipline, heart-to-hearts, questioning, raising his voice, and simply pleading have all been used to foster a change in Jennifer's behavior. Nothing works. At least nothing sustainable.

Jennifer claims that she believes in timelines and accountability when it comes to her staff, but she simply cannot get her own work done. It is just too much. Finally, Dr. Morris decided to work with Jennifer so they could find a solution to her massive time management issue. The seven other principals in his district seemed to be handling their responsibilities quite well. Not only were they completing their tasks, but it seemed as though each of them had a fully functional life with all of the work-life balance to be expected by a public school administrator.

In an attempt to see what was taking up her time, Dr. Morris reported to Jennifer's school to shadow her for a day. He arrived before 7 a.m., and to his surprise Jennifer was already there and engaged in a conversation with a staff member. As Dr. Morris made himself at home in her office, he saw that the conversation was incredibly friendly and meandered from personal matters to work issues and back several times. The meeting ended unceremoniously, and Jennifer looked down and started to reply to an email.

A moment later, Jennifer looked up from her computer and saw Mr. Craig walking by her office; she smiled and asked him to come in for a second. They caught up on their sons' basketball performances before the conversation moved toward an innovative use of technology Jennifer had heard about from a friend in a neighboring district. Mr. Craig thought the idea had merit and said he would look into it. The conversation concluded very professionally.

This cycle repeated over and over again. Parents came in for appointments, and Jennifer would engage them about a random topic. Fifteen minutes later, their conversation was done. A student came in for a scholarship application and 10 minutes later the conversation had touched on the upcoming homecoming dance and boyfriend drama before returning back to the application.

From 7 to 4, Jennifer was in constant motion. She was friendly, sweet, empathetic, and frequently "on brand," sharing a great message that placed students first and focused on progress in every conversation. Jennifer sat down and looked at her computer after work and had 78 emails. She sighed. She was overwhelmed, tired, and looked at Dr. Morris and said, "I will get to these later." Jennifer decided to call it a day.

Communication was not returned, problems were not solved, and suddenly the picture was clear. Jennifer's schedule perfectly matched her priorities, and those priorities perfectly suited Jennifer—but they were not necessarily the priorities of the organization.

To explain, Jennifer was an extrovert and had incredible talent at working with people interpersonally. This is where she excelled. However, she did not take the time to do the things vital to improving the organization. She did not take the time to see work that was beyond her immediate purview. Some of the necessities of the job, such as communication, follow-through, and being a team player, did not register as priorities for her. They didn't excite her and were thus pushed aside. As a result, her mounting to-do list added stress and strained the organization since she was clearly not abiding by the established norms.

Despite all this, she was an incredibly high achiever. It's just that her success could not be sustained. She was under constant stress and was becoming isolated from the rest of her team. Jennifer chose to do what she wanted to do all day, every day. Some of this is great—she led from her strengths—but there is a point of diminishing returns and Jennifer had found it. Her lack of communication about *all* matters that pertained to her role—especially those that she didn't find particularly exciting—was starting to erode her reputation, and she was feeling burned out.

Control

Self-servers do not perceive themselves as selfish—and they're often not. After all, *selfish* is a word loaded with negative connotations. There is a thin line between being driven by selfish desires and simply wanting to have control over your environment. A self-serving employee is typically confident, strong, and passionately opinionated about his or her role within the organization. Many times, self-serving employees had been granted autonomy to build their own job descriptions or were forced to do so as a result of lack of leadership above them. In these situations, they absolutely thrive.

Self-serving employees are decisive, but they can also be considered egocentric and domineering. In the previous scenario, the demands Jennifer places on others to support her school do not correspond to the effort she puts in to supporting anyone else. This runs counter to the characteristics of an ideal team player as one who is humble, hungry, and smart (Lencioni, 2016).

Self-servers attempt to control their environment—sometimes to their own detriment. For example, being able to do what they want may be more important to them than following someone else's suggestion, even though it would make their lives easier. When the desire is to control your own environment, sometimes the most logical directions go unheeded in attempt to forge your own path. In a nutshell, self-servers live up to the idiom: they're more than willing to cut off their nose to spite their face.

In some ways, self-servers are incredibly easy to manage. At their core, they want to be self-reliant. It's important to note that most self-serving workers are not self-serving in the sense that they are on fantasy football or crocheting websites all day. Rather, they want to exert their will on the situation and prove their strength through whatever metric they have decided matters. Larger issues emerge when there is debate as to whether or not their metric is the best one or whether the means to achieve a particular end are appropriate.

If this description defines you, a sense of dread may be settling in because nobody likes to be labeled as controlling. If so, stay resolute; a self-server with altruistic motives is never a bad thing for an organization. In fact, in many cases, it can be a wonderful thing. Troubles arise when the desire to be in control of one's own environment leads to consistent mismanagement of time or feelings of being overwhelmed.

Signs You Are a Self-Server

Very few people characterize themselves as self-serving or controlling. As a result, it is abundantly necessary to read through this section carefully to see if the detailed signs of being a self-server apply to you.

You See Yourself as Different but Equal

Almost everyone reading this has a peer in their organization. No one works in isolation, and I'm sure you see yourself as part of a team larger than yourself. Even if there's only one principal in a school, he or she is still peers with vice principals and on teams with staff, other district leaders, and more.

If you see your peers as the same but different, you may be self-serving. Self-serving employees are usually the first to point out when someone else is not following an organizational norm. However, they do not see a large issue when they ignore the same norm. There may be a good deal of rationalization that takes place to support this perspective. For example, self-servers may think things such as

- "My school is high performing, so the expectations should be changed for me. Why should I need to turn in a monthly update on time like the rest of the principals?"
- "My students have the highest assessment scores. Of course I should have modified expectations for performance. It makes no sense for me to turn in lesson plans when what I'm doing is clearly working."

These types of thoughts are toxic to a work environment and show a lack of self-awareness. Acknowledging and understanding that everyone in an organization, particularly in a school or district, is part of a larger team working toward a unified mission is necessary for ultimate success.

You Are a Challenger

If you exhibit behavior and attitudes toward your direct supervisor that you would never accept from one of your employees, you are probably self-serving. If you challenge new ideas and concepts presented to you that may be fundamentally sound but are not what you want to do, then you are a challenger and probably choosing to challenge in order to exert control over the situation at hand.

For example, it is difficult to argue against the idea that faculty, staff, parents, and students deserve timely feedback. However, if you are self-serving and have the same preferences as Jennifer (which obviously not all self-serving employees will have), you may rebel against a protocol set forth directing that all communication is minimally acknowledged within 24 hours. This is not because you disagree with the premise. You disagree with the premise that someone is going to exert control over how you spend your time or do your job. This makes you a challenger and a self-serving employee.

You Love Authority

People who are self-serving typically feel more comfortable when they are at the helm of a project. This is a pretty simple delineation to consider. Some people have additional stress if they are a part of a team they are not leading. For example, some people find it stressful to be a member of a strategic planning team if they have no direct control over the outcome of the process. Other people experience significant stress when they aren't at the head of the table. Generally speaking, self-servers are far more comfortable owning the authority.

As a result, many people in leadership roles fall into this category. Again, it is important to remember that being self-serving and loving authority does not predetermine that someone will struggle with time management. It does mean, however, that obsessing over control of your own time can lead to a failure to get key components and aspects of your job done.

As a result, self-servers are in a constant struggle and fighting a war on two fronts. On the first, they are working tirelessly to exert control over their own life. On the second, they tend to feel overwhelmed and concerned that they are under pressure and scrutiny to complete the very things they spend so much time and energy rebelling against.

You Can Collaborate . . . Kind Of

If working as part of a team stresses you out, you may be a self-serving employee. This is particularly the case if the idea of working together does not worry you but the actual interaction is intimidating. This is because, if it works appropriately, teamwork is by design a process over which an individual member has no direct control.

This leads to the phenomenon of "collaboration . . . *kind of.*" Everyone has been a part of such an interaction, and honestly, some of us have led these types of processes. They are when the final decision is predetermined and the collaboration is simply a formality or a check box to make everyone feel better about the process. If this is how you lead collaborative efforts, then you probably have at least one trait of a self-serving employee.

Coping Mechanisms

Offload; don't ignore. Everyone has a segment of their job they don't like. For some, it may be returning emails. For others, it may be communicating with parents, writing objectives on the board, or taking minutes at the team meeting. There may be any number of reasons why these types of activities are resisted (e.g., an attempt to set one's own schedule or to assert control), but a bottom line exists. As Marshall Goldsmith (2007) so eloquently put it, "Every decision in your company is made by the person who has the power to make that decision—not necessarily the 'right' person, the 'smartest' person, or the 'best' person" (para. 1).

The point being, there are some components of every job that cannot be improvised or ignored. There are people within each and every organization with the authority to make key decisions that other employees and team members have to live with. Therefore, ignoring expectations and directives is not a useful strategy.

That said, leading and acting on your strengths is a real strategy. For the things you hate doing, do your best to offload as much of the task as possible. Very little in any field, including education, is truly confidential. If a teacher hates making parent contact, use the last three minutes of class once a week to have students email their parents (and cc: you) the following four things: their current grade, if they have any missing assignments, the hardest concept explored during the week, and the best thing that happened in class.

Bam! Two problems solved at once. That's more than 20 parent emails completed in three minutes, with students owning their own progress, and a simple fix to fill the void of the last three minutes of class that often lead to disruptive behavior and stress.

This is one simple example, but the point can be extrapolated. In education, so much of what we do can be shared with our students. Not only does this free you up to do what you are best at, but it also empowers students and often teaches them additional skills. Common examples of this include student-led parent conferences, student-created newsletters, and student leaders taking ownership of any number of different classroom roles and responsibilities.

If you don't have the autonomy to create all elements of your workday specifically to your liking (and you don't, unless you are a self-employed entrepreneur), then find creative ways to offload the tasks that weigh you down.

Seek to understand. I have been around a lot of bosses in my work as a consultant. In this work, I have rubbed shoulders with some of the finest leaders in America's schools. I have also seen instances of educational and leadership malpractice. Even in the very worst scenarios, I very rarely find a boss, manager, or leader who intentionally gives out tasks and work without some sort of thoughtful rationale.

To be clear, this does not make the rationale accurate or sound, but the reason is almost always not to annoy the principals, teachers, or support staff. This is an important point to make, because when work is heaped on us, it becomes easy to reject both the task and the person assigning the work. This is often when the desire to control creeps in and those tasks get avoided or go ignored.

The strategy to combat this is simple. Seek to understand why you are being asked to do something. If you hate the task but understand the purpose, then you are much less likely to want to exert control over the situation. These five simple questions can help move you from a self-server to a team player if you ask them with the true intent of seeking to understand:

- Why are we doing this?
- Does this align with our mission and vision?
- Does this support our stated goals?
- Does this replace any other work we are currently doing?
- Is this coming from somewhere we cannot control (e.g., a new state regulation)?

Ideally, a great leader would answer all of these questions when making "the ask," but we know that is not always the case. Thus, working through these five questions can help ensure that someone who is typically self-serving knows the purpose and rationale of the work they are being asked to do. Moreover, if you can clearly see the rationale for the behavior you are avoiding, then asking yourself these questions can prove to be beneficial. It can also reveal where your resistance isn't grounded in reality. For example, it's clear that reaching out and partnering with parents hits the first three questions with an affirmative response. Recognizing that, it's hard to argue with the purpose of the task, even if it's not something you enjoy doing.

Ask for options. Personalities are funny things. The desire to control may be so deeply ingrained that you need to feel at least a small sense of autonomy. In that case, asking for an option may be all that is needed to allow you to feel comfortable with a task. This may be as simple as completing a task in Google Drive instead of emailing an attachment. Although these differences don't seem like much, they can help us gain confidence that we are in control of our own time and effort.

I encourage you to think of how much more enjoyable a conference is when you get to choose the breakout sessions you will attend. There's a huge difference, right? The desire for a perception of control plays itself out with my oldest son constantly. If I tell him to clean his room, fold his laundry, and take out the garbage, we have a full-fledged fight. However, if I give him the same chores but tell him they need to get done before he goes to bed, there is no issue. By giving him some choice, I can avoid all the conflict.

Solutions

Lasting change happens only through intense and intentional effort. If your core desire at work (on a personal level) is to ensure that you have control over your environment, time, and job description, then it will take significant effort for you to adjust your behaviors. This section provides some suggestions that—with the appropriate amount of work—can lead to lasting and productive change.

Understand That Control Is Sometimes About Needs—Not Wants

Control is not simply a desire but also a need. Some biologists assert that the deepest need people have is for a sense of control. So if you have been reading this and it resonates, it is probably because there is a biological and evolutionary reason it does. A key element to understanding our desire for control is that the deep need is for *a sense of control*, not just for control.

This may help people grasp the concept differently. This is not just about power; it has a significantly wider scope. Psychologists often point to apparently irrational behavior from people who suffer from terminal illnesses or who have feelings of personal oppression. These actions are believed to manifest from a sense of powerlessness and a personal lack of control—whether that's real or perceived.

The evolutionary viewpoint is straightforward. When we are in control of our environment, we have a better chance at survival (Changing Minds, 2018). Thus, the desire for control has been genetically programmed into our DNA for thousands of years. Which begs the question, how does this help me get over my need for control and the potential angst it is causing me at work?

Luckily, there are a few things we can do to work to feed our biological need for control while also increasing our productivity.

- **Work for certainty.** Our root desire for control is because we want to ensure that we are safe and secure. Exert control over the outcomes of your actions, and the internal desire for total control will ease.

- **Decrease stress.** Stress increases our natural tendency to desire control. When responsibilities and tasks remain on the to-do list, we buckle down and attempt to control whatever we can at that moment. This is a natural reaction. The best way to reduce your desire for control is to return to equilibrium. You need to get your head above water. Do whatever it takes to get back to a place of minimum stress, and the desire to control everything should dissipate.

- **Think of Maslow.** As educators, we are well-versed in Maslow's hierarchy of needs. We cannot do incredible things at work when our basic needs are not being met. Feeling psychologically and emotionally safe are core needs, and we must get there before we can get on with more complex work (i.e., Maslow before Bloom). In other words, our internal desire for control needs to be fed in order to move forward toward greater work, greater productivity, and greater time management.

Use Time Management to Maintain Control

Everybody has heard the saying "They won the battle but lost the war." If you are fighting to exert control over your daily routine and thereby creating a monumental logjam of work for yourself, then that is exactly what you are doing. You may be winning the immediate battle, but you are losing the war. There is no easier and simpler way to put it: the most valuable thing you can control is your time. Time is your autonomy.

Sometimes you need to do the grunt work so you can enjoy the rest of your time without stress or interruption. In the example that began this chapter, Jennifer's desire to control her time at work meant that she was missing out on time she could be enjoying at home. Time to work on herself, enjoy her family, practice her faith, and contribute to her physical well-being disappeared because of her desire to exhibit control over what she wanted when she wanted as an employee.

Practice Empathy

People often lose their ability to be empathetic when they are focused on maintaining control of a situation. This frequently leads to regret over one's actions or the decisions they make at a given time. For instance, not following an organizational norm of acknowledging communication within 24 hours may not seem like a big deal if it doesn't align with your personal preferences on communication. Irrespective of mandate or norm, though, empathy should dictate that we communicate better and more responsively to our peers and customers. Here are three quick examples that happen frequently in schools where people do not employ empathy when it comes to communication:

- **Principal to principal:** Can you let me know if my choir can use your gym on April 3rd for a concert?
- **Teacher to principal:** I am having some trouble with Brandon in class. Can we brainstorm some ideas?
- **Parent to teacher:** I am concerned with Johnny's grades right now. Can you let me know what is going on and how we can help him?

All three are perfectly legitimate requests. None is urgent or requires immediate attention. All three, however, are most likely providing stress and angst to the person who made the request. Still, items such as these often sit for far too long in an email inbox and do not receive attention as the recipient attempts to exert control over his or her own work environment. The simple act of taking one minute to put yourself in the other party's shoes would trigger a response. Empathy is key to not acting in a self-serving, control-hungry manner at work.

Here are three quick practices you can use to strengthen your empathy muscles:

- **Ask.** We often overlook the most reliable method when learning how to employ empathy. Empathy is the ability to place yourself emotionally in someone else's shoes. So it is perfectly appropriate to ask someone how they feel, what their viewpoint is, or how they would react if the situation were reversed. Empathy is undoubtedly a skill, but it is something within all of us. Taking the proactive step of asking someone forces us to a place where empathy is more emotionally accessible.

- **Listen to understand.** We often listen to reply. We listen to fix. We listen in order to be heard. Practicing empathy means listening to understand. It is difficult to practice empathy when we're listening to reply because the perspective never shifts. Once you take the time to look at a situation through someone else's lens (by listening to them), empathy becomes much more natural.

- **Use simple phrases.** Employing the following three phrases in your conversations will force you to practice empathy: (1) What I believe I am hearing you say is . . . ; (2) If I understand the situation from your perspective, it is . . . ; (3) In your mind, what is the ideal resolution . . . ? By intentionally leveraging these three phrases, you are forced to employ empathy in every conversation. Although sustained change is made by thinking your way into new behavior, sometimes forcing new behaviors into your old routine is a great way to make it through the transitional stage.

Yield Control Intentionally

Sometimes, the best strategy is to lean into the task that is befuddling you. If you realize that you are attempting to exert control over every situation, then it may be time to intentionally yield control. This is tricky, because as with everything, moderation is key. If you truly value control, giving it all up will be a shock to the system. That said, systematically allowing yourself and your time to be directed in areas that make the most sense may be the best option to help create lasting change within yourself.

A few years ago, I was working with a principal who was struggling with control. The heart and soul of his leadership style was a complex and comprehensive improvement strategy. I had encouraged him for years to yield some of the process because he was the only driver. If he were to ever leave, the process would have folded in upon itself. He never did.

Finally, after working with his supervisor, we banned him from the project. He was incapable of gradually releasing responsibility. The baby steps were never taken and progress was never made. We ripped the bandage for him. It was painful, but he survived. So too did the improvement planning process. It was not perfect, but it was sufficient. He learned that he overvalued himself and was only serving his needs by holding so tightly to the leadership of the plan. For years, he had convinced himself that his controlling ways were in the school's best interest. It took a radical action for him to learn this lesson and begin to change his behaviors.

Realign Your Mission

If your personal mission does not align to the work you are doing to achieve the organizational mission, then you will never be happy in your job. A lack of happiness will trigger the desire to assert additional control over what you are doing. This is a vicious and endless cycle. Said succinctly, if your personal mission, vision, and values do not align with those of your organization, you should probably find a different organization.

At first blush, it may seem difficult not to have a personal mission that aligns with what a school is trying to accomplish. There is nothing further from the truth. Some schools believe deeply in technology, others in student voice and leadership, and others focus deeply on social justice. I will tell you from a very real place, there are many educators who are not on board with any of those platforms. You know it in your soul. There are good fits and bad fits. When your brain tells your gut that this is a bad fit, you should listen.

Final Thoughts

Seeking control is normal. Seeking control over your daily work to the point of time management stress is not normal. The good news is that with self-awareness and reflection, there are many strategies to improve. The bottom line is that the desire to have some control and autonomy is normal, but if you are seeking control to the point that it is actually making you less effective and efficient, then it is definitely time to make some personal changes.

8

Perpetually Imbalanced

As I write this, I am overweight and out of shape. It happens every time I find myself in a writing groove. When this book is complete, it will be my fourth book in 18 months. I got into a groove. I loved every minute of it. Zero regrets.

What seems to happen with me, however, is that I cannot find a perfect balance—or at least a perfect balance for me. I know we all talk about it: the perfect life, the idealized version of what we are supposed to be—great parents, wonderful spouses, the friend everyone wants to have, wildly successful in our careers, at peace in our faith, and healthy stewards of our bodily vessels. How about you? Have you found a perfect balance? For me, that balance is a goal I have never quite been able to reach.

I seem to have just enough time and energy to write and speak or to run and lift weights. It's either one or the other. I can keep everything else constant, but not those two. Those are the variables. Those are the things for which I am either all in or all out. Here's the thing, though. I love doing both of them, and I'm happier when I am doing them.

This led me to think about balance in a different light than I previously did. I work with many principals and teachers who struggle with balance. The truth is that being perpetually imbalanced negatively affects your ability to get the most important things done, which gives the impression that this is a time management issue. As we've seen over and over again throughout this book, this is a misdiagnosis.

This chapter explores issues of balance and provides suggestions and solutions to help people find balance and better manage their time. In an effort to help everyone understand their own priorities and their own imbalance, I have synthesized the component areas people explain to me as vitally important but that sometimes fall out of sync when attempting to find balance. They are family, friends, faith, finance, fitness, and profession. I refer to them it as the five *F*s and a *P*.

Five *F*s and a *P*

Family

Family first is something you often hear people say. Family first is something you occasionally see people live. The challenge when trying to manage your time is that many of these six components are intertwined and at times ambiguous. For instance, if it truly is family first and you have the opportunity to do some side work to gain additional income or attend your child's 2nd grade concert, what do you choose?

The answer is that there is no answer. Context matters. This is what makes time management so difficult and leads people to feel as though they are in perpetual imbalance. I work with one principal who is a dedicated mother and does more for her children than most parents I know. Still, she feels constant guilt because of the time her job demands.

What is important and consistent throughout the exploration of these six components is that perception drives the work far more than fact. Your perception is your reality, regardless of the facts. It is impossible to quantify how much time you need to dedicate to your family in order to be a successful father, mother, or spouse. Moreover, there is often disequilibrium between what we perceive is necessary and what is truly needed to fill your loved one's proverbial cup.

My father worked day and night to provide the type of life he thought his family deserved. As a result, there were a few nights a week when my father would not come home until very late since he was finishing off a 16-hour shift at the factory. Those times when my father was not around did not negatively affect how I viewed him or his contribution to our family. It did just the opposite. It taught me to put family before self and that the most important thing I needed to do was work to provide my children with a better life than the one that was provided to me.

That being said, the exact same scenario could have been internalized in a very different manner by someone else. It is ambiguous, and the world is contextual. My point is that we are often chasing a moving target that we have arbitrarily established for ourselves.

Friends

It is always interesting to me what fills people's buckets. I know some people who value their friends on the same level of importance as any other category described in this chapter. What's important to them may not align to what's important to me. And the fact that we are so different is perfectly normal. Embracing this perspective is vital in understanding others and their search for balance. Understanding that what others need, you may not—and vice versa—is key to having successful interpersonal relationships and is vital if you are attempting to lead others.

Last year, I spent a good amount of time counseling a friend who was separated from his wife. We spent several weeks talking through their issues in order to help him hopefully resolve the issues that were tarnishing their union. The root problem was that my friend loved his friends and valued his ability to interact and spend time with them as much as his wife valued her time with her extended family. Both husband and wife in this circumstance were annoyed by their partner's lack of commitment to what they enjoyed and by their rationale as to why they enjoyed spending their individual time in the manner they did.

After about two months apart, the two finally engaged in this meaningful discussion. They came to a deeper understanding of what made each other happy. They both agreed that they needed to adapt their personal behaviors to be a better partner to each other while at the same time adjusting their perspectives and better supporting their partner's desire to spend time with whomever they wanted.

The point is that we do not get to choose other people's priorities. We get the unique opportunity as humans to think critically about our priorities and to act accordingly. Such is the dilemma with friends and finding balance. Friendships are often one of the first things to be thrown away in search of finding balance in the other areas, but for some people, they are vitally important to well-being and peace of mind. If you find yourself feeling perpetually imbalanced, the role of key friendships is an important concept to explore. You may be undervaluing their role in your happiness—or just as easily overvaluing their role.

Faith

Faith is incredibly important to a vast number of people. For many, it is their primary area of importance. Faith is the key lever that moves them forward. Faith has the power to lift us up, unite or divide us, and provide hope for the future for many people. People exhibit and experience their faith in so many different ways it is impossible to capture in simple text. For the sake of this work, I simply define faith as the level of spirituality that someone needs to nurture within themselves to become their best selves.

I have a colleague who considers himself immensely spiritual and finds time to tend to his spirit on long walks in his woods. I have another dear friend who feels he does not do his duty if he doesn't spend multiple hours per week in his place of worship. I also have friends who are high-ranking officers in their church but embrace the idea that there is a thin line between Saturday night and Sunday morning. And I have friends who do not recognize faith in their life at all, yet their actions are incredibly giving and they have very moral and charitable souls.

The point is that faith manifests itself in different ways, but for many people, a life without faith is a life without balance. Unfortunately, faith does not have bill collectors, bosses, or another tangible accountability metric. So when I go around and talk to people about being truly fulfilled and living the life they have imagined, many people recognize that they are not spiritually fulfilled. Thereby, their life is imbalanced.

Finance

I don't believe money is the key to happiness. However, I do believe that not having the means to live the life you desire is a very real cause of stress. This is true for anyone, but it is particularly so for educators. To be clear, choosing to enter the world of education as a teacher means you are submitting to a finite cap on your earning potential (at least in your primary occupation). Teaching is the only college-educated profession (outside of seminary) where this seems to be the case.

We live in a time when public schools in America are held up to a higher standard than ever before, are significantly underfunded in most states, and are consistently criticized in both the media and the political arena. Couple that with poor salaries and we are staring down an inevitable teacher shortage of catastrophic proportions in the coming years. In short, money matters.

It matters to each and every one of us, and if money is not right, almost nothing else matters in terms of finding balance. Earlier in this chapter, I discussed the natural push and pull of these six key components to finding a work-life balance. When money isn't right, the rest goes out the window. If the mortgage payment is late, chances are that stress is mounting and stagnating efforts in every other area. In addition, far too many educators today are forced to spend time on a "side hustle" to make up the income—which means personal balance is nearly impossible.

Fitness

As I said, this is the one area I need to focus on more. I know that I have to do a better job at maintaining my health and fitness. I cannot be more blunt—you have just one life. You have just one body. You have just one vessel to carry you forward and help you achieve everything you want out of life. There is no balance without health.

If you think I am overstating it, think of someone in your life who has battled cancer. As a two-time cancer survivor, I can assure you that nothing else matters when that is the battle at hand. Big problems become small. Financial wants become wishes. Only one thing matters: surviving the battle. It is unfortunate that for many of us, our wellness tends to be set aside until it becomes an emergency.

I am encouraged by the recognition of this in the education community; many schools and districts are moving toward wellness models for all the right reasons. Teaching and being a building leader is an exhausting and demanding profession. There is simply no way to take care of others unless you are taking care of yourself. I applaud leaders in this realm, namely Adam Welcome and the #RunLAP crew who are inspiring people to face the challenge of taking care of themselves. This is a necessary stance for those in education to take.

Profession

It is difficult to be a great educator without putting in the time. Like any other profession, there are some rare individuals who have insane talent and are able to do great things without putting in a ton of time, but for the rest of us mere mortals, education is a beast of a job.

It's not just about the time. It's also the emotional energy it takes to care for and love the children you serve and the staff you serve them with. It's taking home their problems. It's having the conversation in bed with your significant other and saying, "If I could just take him home." It's the ever-changing content and standards educators are supposed to shoot for in order to be effective. It's the standardized assessments.

The world is a rapidly and permanently changing place, and schools are—by and large—hesitant to and fearful of change. That's not a great combination, to be sure. We don't have a clue what our kids will be asked to do in the future. So it's frustrating when change is enacted, it is slow and often fraught with process errors. We are seemingly fighting an uphill battle.

My perspective is simple: we have two options. We can wish for the world around us to stop changing, or we can work to change ourselves. If our mission is to best serve the students we see each day, then that choice is elementary (pun intended). The work will never be done for us. Our balance will always be strained if we are working to do the absolute best we can on behalf of kids every day. We might be fighting an uphill battle, but it's absolutely a battle worth fighting.

Signs You Are Perpetually Imbalanced

For most people, this is simply a given. There is a constant struggle to be the best version of ourselves. The best version of us allows for true inner peace and happiness. There is no definitive metric to explore this; it is as simple as how you feel.

You Feel Constant Guilt

Almost everyone experiences guilt from time to time. We often blame others for making us feel guilty, but the truth is that guilt is simply an emotion we all feel. Freud (1930/2010) attempted to explain guilt as an innate feeling everyone feels because we know how truly awful our most awful thoughts, feelings, and desires are. It's something we must own and try to understand as part of our deeper self-awareness.

Guilt is a frequent partner for the perpetually imbalanced. The reason is that our actions most often align with our desires, so when there is a disconnect between what we want to do and what we believe we *should be* doing, guilt ensues. For those who struggle to find balance, this is an exceptionally common occurrence.

I think of my wife when I think of someone who feels enormous guilt anytime they do anything for themselves. I'm not just referring to things like spa days; I also mean work, time with friends, or even visiting with family. She is so compelled to be an incredible mother that any time she has the option to be with kids and chooses something else, she feels intense guilt. If this scenario rings true to you, chances are you are living in perpetual imbalance.

You Often Feel Discomfort

Discomfort comes from acting on what you think you should be doing and ignoring other aspects of your life that are important to you. This may result from spending six hours on the weekend driving for Uber and missing your daughter's softball game. Or it could be the feeling that comes from staying home with the kids for the third consecutive day and missing a long-overdue jog with friends.

Discomfort manifests in many different ways, but it is clearly our brain trying to help us find balance. With increased self-awareness comes increased responsibility to attend to what our body, brain, and soul need. No single person can be everything to everyone. Discomfort arises when we desperately try to be what we *think* others want us to be without listening to what we know we need to fill our own bucket and find balance.

You Are Constantly Running on Empty

Exhaustion manifests for several reasons. In no way do I mean to assert that everyone who is currently running on empty is suffering from an issue of imbalance. I would argue, however, that if you have felt like you are running on empty for an extended period of time and have had a full medical check-up that does not provide a reason why, then you may be suffering from a significant imbalance.

Too often, we believe we can work our way through an imbalance. Instead of addressing the fact that there does not seem to be enough time in the day, we neglect our self-care, sleep, and a variety of other issues. This is a self-perpetuating problem. As our exhaustion continues to mount, we become less effective and efficient in what we are trying to get done. This extends beyond our professional life. Think about it; is it high-quality family time if you are nodding off every five minutes?

If you are always on the go and exhausted, the problem isn't your effort. The problem is that you haven't figured out how to balance all of the things you need to get done versus the important things you should be doing. The mental task of analyzing the circumstances and developing solutions is important in order to provide a potential solution to the issue of being perpetually imbalanced.

Coping Mechanisms

Calendarize your work areas. There is a decent chance you have never thought of your life balance in the context of the six areas detailed in this chapter. Now that you have, don't waste the opportunity to plot out your life based on these areas. It seems straightforward, but it may be a bit more complex than you think.

This is not as simple as blocking out time on your calendar for all six areas. Well, maybe it is, but that strategy is most likely not going to be sustainable. My suggestion would be to calendarize your day. During the times you are not living meeting to meeting or class to class, make an intentional effort to chart down how you spend your time. With a digital calendar, this takes literally 10 seconds. Try it for just one week. This exercise will allow you to see where you spend a majority of your time. The results in most cases will not be shocking, but looking at the data will force you to confront the brutal facts.

Most people find that a majority of their time is spent working toward their profession. This leads to a logical question: Why do people stay in jobs that drain their buckets? If your work is not rewarding to you in a significant manner, then perhaps that is the first realization that needs to take place. If not, a cycle of hopelessness will at some point undoubtedly begin.

Second, there will be complete voids. To explain, there will be things we say are important to us, such as fitness, that literally receive zero minutes of attention throughout the course of a week. Remember, our schedules reflect our priorities. If fitness is a stated priority, but you cannot find time to do the work, then it probably isn't really a priority for you. A mental shift has to take place before the physical shift has an opportunity for lasting success.

The intent of working through a calendar approach is for you to realize where you currently are. Once you realize where you are and how many minutes each week are spent doing things like social media and decompressing, obvious opportunities begin to present themselves. In that 30 minutes after dinner when the kids go to their rooms and your spouse typically takes a shower, you could crank out 50 squats, 50 push-ups, and 50 sit-ups instead of having a glass of wine and scrolling through Facebook.

I imagine this is a trade-off most of us would make if we actually took the time think about what fulfills us.

Stop living for the weekends. If you survive the week to love the weekend, your balance is most likely totally off. If you wait to think about family, faith, fitness, or finance until Saturday, then your work-life balance is corrupted. The question that begs to be asked is whether you are so consumed with your profession that no other time exists—or if you are spending your time away from work distracted by work but not working to get better.

To explain, many people come home from work and are stressed out. They simply veg on the couch, eat their stress away, or mindlessly scroll through social media as a means of coping. Then, Saturday rolls around and they want to spend time with their family, clean the house, balance the checkbook, and fit in a run. If all goes well, they go shopping and maybe schedule something fun like a movie on Sunday. This sounds like far too many of our lives.

If we wait to address the other core areas of our life until the weekend, balance will never exist. Balance is as much about time management as it is about filling our bucket. It is worth repeating that, as educators, it is very difficult to take care of others if we are not taking care of ourselves. Likewise, when we neglect to find balance in our lives, it is nearly impossible to take care of ourselves.

Ask for expectations. Balance is lost on many people because of the expectations they place on themselves for other people. To explain, if you think your family needs you to sit with them and watch television, you may force yourself to do so. While sitting next to your family, you may be completely distracted because you'd rather be running, meditating, or preparing for the next day's meeting. Now imagine they don't view this time as valuable. Does anything change?

It does for most people, and most (even healthy) couples and families have never had this conversation. The conversation alone does not mean that your personal expectations will change, but it means you are working toward aligning your behaviors with your intended outcomes. For example, I take my two oldest sons to breakfast at least once a week, usually on Wednesdays. This is the most valuable time I spend with them all week. The hour we spend at breakfast equates to five hours on the couch next to them after school, and it makes up for the nights I am out of town on business or stuck in meetings late into the night.

This nonnegotiable hour we spend together every week means more to my sons than five arbitrarily spent hours where we happen to occupy the same room. This is incredibly liberating for me and allows me to spend time finding balance in other areas. Remember, we all have the same 24 hours per day; those who are extremely effective and have balance just use that time more wisely.

Be present when present. Balance is much more achievable if you are truly present in the activity in which you are partaking. "Family time" on the couch watching television while you scroll through your phone is not exactly being present. Sitting in the pew at church but not really listening to the message is not being present. Going to the gym and working out at a rate that doesn't tax your body is not being present.

This mental task of being present in all that you do will transform your interactions and engagement level. Relationships will improve. Balance will emerge. Time on task will seem like a reward instead of a punishment. This may be the simplest coping mechanism I can recommend for the perpetually imbalanced. Switch on your mental capacity to be one with the activity you are already doing.

Audit the people in your life. Let's face it; some people are simply time and energy drainers. If you have people in your life who are negatively contributing to your mindset, health, and well-being, you need to make an adjustment. In life, people are either fillers or drainers. Don't let yourself be surrounded by drainers; live the life you have imagined for yourself—not the one others are trying to place on you. Remember, people's reactions to the events of their life are directly related to their worldview. Don't surround yourself with negative people.

Solutions

I'm not positive anybody will ever get this perfectly right. Balance is the goal, but it is an ever-moving target we all continue to chase. However, the processes articulated in this section provide the best chance to achieve this incredibly elusive goal. In some cases, they give us permission to understand that balance may not be everyone's goal.

Embrace the Cost of Greatness

Olympic gymnasts spend vast quantities of time away from their families while children in order to pursue their goal. Michael Jordan's and Kobe Bryant's fanatical drive to be the best is legendary. Steve Jobs was noticeably absent as a father as he struggled to build Apple. Elon Musk proudly states that he worked over 100 hours per week for 15 years while building his empire. Greatness requires atypical balance.

Let me be clear, balance is whatever *you* define balance to be. If your inner peace is not going to be met without being great at something, then there is an above-average chance that your life is not going to look like everyone else's. The six components of balance as discussed in this chapter will not be met. Therefore, if your desire is to be an all-time great, then you will need to work like an all-time great. This is true in many realms. If you are going to be the greatest dad in the world, then you may not have time to be the best friend possible. If you are going to be the best wife in the world, then you may not be the best principal in the world. Greatness has a price.

Embracing the cost of greatness is necessary. The reason for the cost is because there is a cognitive dissonance between what people think they want and what they are willing to sacrifice in order to achieve it. The question becomes: Does this disconnect breed unhappiness? Are you fundamentally unhappy because you believe you could be Teacher of the Year and on the keynote circuit if you just had more time to give? Do you feel stifled by your family responsibilities? If so, you have not wrestled with the cost of greatness and come to a personal realization that will allow you to chart a path to the life you want.

Find Your Lever

When working through the elements required to create balance, many people wonder how it's possible to fit more into the day. It is vital to realize that many of the elements you're currently missing actually serve to create space and happiness rather than the opposite. For instance, it is entirely possible that by committing to going to bed an hour earlier and waking up an hour earlier so you have time to work out, the other component areas of your life will see a boost.

Working out and taking care of your fitness is just one example. For others, taking care of themselves spiritually might be the most important thing they could do. As a result of feeling at peace within themselves, their ability to be an outstanding mother, father, son, daughter, teacher, principal, or friend improves exponentially. Likewise, if you put in the work to get your financial life in order, then the stress reduction that comes from that change may allow you to be more present while interacting with your children or make you a better teammate to your colleagues at work.

Somewhere in each of our lives, we have that figurative lever we can pull to fill our bucket and improve our life. The key to finding balance is acknowledging which of the six areas described in this chapter helps bring life and energy to the other areas and then dedicating time to nurturing it. For me, reading and being alone with my thoughts is the best possible way for me to reenergize. Realizing this has allowed me not only to improve professionally but also to refocus on being a better husband and father.

Find your lever. Once you find it, be brave enough to pull it and acknowledge what you need to be the best you. Then make the conscious choice of doing what it takes to fill your bucket.

Make Balance a Conscious Choice

Balance does not just happen for most people; if it did, there would be no point in writing this chapter. When I sit down with educators and ask what is missing from their life or what they wish they could do more of, I have yet to hear anybody say, "Nothing." This means, very clearly, that people are struggling to find balance.

When people tell me they wish they could spend more time with their family, be better at their job, or travel more, I respond by asking what is stopping them. That question is usually met with a litany of responses. I pause and then ask, "So what is *really* stopping you?" Their answers always come down to one thing: they are stopping themselves.

Our lives are a sum of the choices we make. Some of you have been dealt more difficult hands than others, but we all have the choice every day to decide how to move forward. This conversation is much bigger than simply finding balance, but balance is a clear part of the dialogue. If you find a fundamental lack of balance in your life, make a conscious choice to change—and then take action. The world, and more precisely your world, is never ever going to change on its own. You must exhibit an internal locus of control and take control of your life in all aspects in order to find balance.

Final Thoughts

Trying to be all things to all people is a recipe for personal disaster. Happiness erodes as you continue to play a guessing game that only you know you are playing. As a result, you become mediocre in many areas, stressed out, and feel like you are constantly struggling to stay above water. We've all been there. The good news is that these situations are not permanent and we all have the ability and power to take back control of our lives. This chapter was designed to provide a framework to help you chart a path toward the life you have imagined. You control so much more than you think. Increased efficiency and time management are just two of the many things that await if you are willing to engage in this extremely difficult conversation with yourself.

9

Conclusion

The thesis of this book is simple: there is no such thing as a time management issue. Time management issues are the symptom, not the cause. The issue that persists for many when they are unable to do what is required of them is undoubtedly something different than a time management issue. This book attempted to articulate eight different reasons that are true triggers for that symptom. In each of the eight areas, I presented coping mechanisms and solutions we can all work toward.

My true hope in writing this book is that people will take the time to self-analyze why they, or those they lead, struggle at being efficient and effective in their jobs. It has become too easy for people to blame time management as an issue when it is really just a symptom of a larger problem. The goal is that people can take the coping mechanisms and solutions provided and chart a path that is more comfortable for them to lead. Nobody enjoys being known as the person who cannot get things done on time. This book is designed to provide a path forward for those looking to help themselves and for those looking to coach others through this problem.

The chart in Figure 9.1 outlines the root issues, coping mechanisms, and solutions that were presented throughout the book.

Figure 9.1

Causes, Coping Mechanisms, and Solutions

Root Cause	Coping Mechanisms	Solutions
Work Avoidant	• Eat the big frog first. • Make sure your calendar matches your priorities. • Schedule flextime. • Seek out an accountability partner.	• Focus on skill acquisition. • Hone your grit. • Align your priorities. • Gain confidence. • Engage in self-monitoring.
People Pleaser	• Just say *no*. • Ask for time. • Determine who benefits most.	• Identify your purpose. • Focus on healthy relationships. • Clarify your vision. • Depersonalize.
Prisoner of the Moment	• Write down daily goals. • Finish first. • Dig deep daily. • Create visual reminders to maintain focus on the most important thing.	• Seek to understand your brain. • Train your brain. • Take smart breaks and track progress.
Checklist Dependent	• Disaggregate your to-do list from email. • Use a commitment device. • Reduce to seven.	• Understand the dopamine rush. • Make if-then lists. • Determine complexity, time-lines, and importance. • Create lists that match your priorities.
Disorganized	• Reduce paper. • Force a relocation. • Mitigate the impact of your disorganization.	• Understand the real issue. • Strategize for the long term. • Develop an information triumvirate.
Technology Avoidant	• Create nonnegotiables for yourself. • Be strategic and gradual in your adoption. • Abandon the "pencil problem" myth. • Remember that it is not "one more thing."	• Admit the value of technology. • Invest in your growth. • Find a buddy.

continued

Figure 9.1

Causes, Coping Mechanisms, and Solutions (*continued*)

Root Cause	Coping Mechanisms	Solutions
Self-Server	• Offload; don't ignore. • Seek to understand. • Ask for options.	• Understand that control is sometimes about needs—not wants. • Use time management to maintain control. • Practice empathy. • Yield control intentionally. • Realign your mission.
Perpetually Imbalanced	• Calendarize your work areas. • Stop living for the weekends. • Ask for expectations. • Be present when present. • Audit the people in your life.	• Embrace the cost of greatness. • Find your lever. • Make balance a conscious choice.

I am incredibly excited that you took the time and mental energy to read this book. Nothing great happens for us without an intentional effort and energy put forth to improve ourselves. That is truly the secret to success and happiness. I hope this book helps you move from whatever your status quo has become to the best version of you.

Just keep leading.

References

Barrabi, T. (2017). March madness 2018: U.S. companies will lose billions to slacking workers. *Fox Business*. Retrieved from www.foxbusiness.com/features/march-madness-2018-u-s-companies-will-lose-billions-to-slacking-workers

Changing Minds. (2018). Evolution. *ChangingMinds.org*. Retrieved from http://changingminds.org/explanations/evolution/evolution.htm

Chapman University. (2015). What Americans fear most: Chapman University's second annual survey of American fears released [blog post]. Retrieved from *Chapman University Press Room* at https://blogs.chapman.edu/press-room/2015/10/13/what-americans-fear-most-chapman-universitys-second-annual-survey-of-american-fears-released

Chunn, L. (2017). The psychology of the to-do list: Why your brain loves ordered tasks. *The Guardian*. Retrieved from www.theguardian.com/lifeandstyle/2017/may/10/the-psychology-of-the-to-do-list-why-your-brain-loves-ordered-tasks

Clancy, K. (2014, July 10). Your brain is on the brink of chaos: Neurological evidence for chaos in the nervous system is growing. *Nautilus, 15*. Retrieved from http://nautil.us/issue/15/turbulence/your-brain-is-on-the-brink-of-chaos

Consortium for School Networking. (2008). Learning to change: Changing to Learn [Video]. *YouTube*. Retrieved from www.youtube.com/watch?v=tahTKdEUAPk

Covey, S. R. (2004). *The 7 habits of highly effective people: Restoring the character ethic*. New York: Free Press.

Duckworth, A. (2016). *Grit: The power of passion and perseverance*. New York: Scribner.

Dweck, C. S. (2006). *Mindset: The new psychology of success*. New York: Random House.

Frankel, L. P. (2004). *Nice girls don't get the corner office: 101 unconscious mistakes women make that sabotage their careers*. New York: Warner Business.

Freud, S. (1930/2010). *Civilization and its discontents*. New York: W. W. Norton.

Gladwell, M. (2008). *Outliers: The story of success*. New York: Little, Brown.

Goldsmith, M. (2007, November 5). How to influence decision makers. *Harvard Business Review*. Retrieved from https://hbr.org/2007/11/how-to-influence-decision-make

Goldsmith, M., & Reiter, M. (2015). *Triggers: Creating behavior that lasts—becoming the person you want to be*. New York: Crown Business.

Gregoire, C. (2013, September 15). The science of conquering your fears—and living a more courageous life. *Huffington Post*. Retrieved from www.huffingtonpost.com/2013/09/15/conquering-fear_n_3909020.html

Harvard Medical School. (2018). Understanding the stress response: Chronic activation of this survival mechanism impairs health. *Harvard Health Publishing*. Retrieved from www.health.harvard.edu/staying-healthy/understanding-the-stress-response

Iyengar, S., & Lepper, M. (2000). When choice is demotivating: Can one desire too much of a good thing? *Journal of Personality and Social Psychology, 79*, 995–1006.

Jiang, J. (2016). What I learned from 100 days of rejection [Video]. *TED: Ideas Worth Spreading*. Retrieved from www.ted.com/talks/jia_jiang_what_i_learned_from_100_days_of_rejection/footnotes?referrer=playlist-the_line_between_success_and_f

Khoury, B., Sharma, M., Rush, S. E., & Fournier, C. (2015). Mindfulness-based stress reduction for healthy individuals: A meta-analysis. *Journal of Psychosomatic Research, 78*(6), 519–528.

Kruze, K. (2015, July 10). Millionaires don't use to-do lists. *Forbes*. Retrieved from www.forbes.com/sites/kevinkruse/2015/07/10/to-do-lists-time-management/#36296c7f4413

LaFrance, A. (2015, March 30). When people feared computers. *The Atlantic*. Retrieved from www.theatlantic.com/technology/archive/2015/03/when-people-feared-computers/388919

Lencioni, P. (2016). *The ideal team player: How to recognize and cultivate three essential virtues*. New York: Jossey-Bass.

Livingstone, L. (2009). Eight key attributes of effective leaders: Words of advice from top business executives. *Graziadio Business Review, 12*(4). Retrieved from https://gbr.pepperdine.edu/2010/08/eight-key-attributes-of-effective-leaders

Markovitz. (2012, January 24). To-do lists don't work. *Harvard Business Review*. Retrieved from https://hbr.org/2012/01/to-do-lists-dont-work

Masicampo, E. J., & Baumeister, R. F. (2011). Consider it done! Plan making can eliminate the cognitive effects of unfulfilled goals. *Journal of Personality and Social Psychology, 101*(4), 667–683.

Meyer, U., & Coffey, W. R. (2015). *Above the line: Lessons in leadership and life from a championship season*. New York: Penguin.

Muhammad, A. (2010). *Transforming school culture: How to overcome staff division*. Bloomington, IN: Solution Tree.

Qualman, E. (2017). Socialnomics 2017 [Video]. *YouTube*. Retrieved from www.youtube.com/watch?v=PWa8-43kE-Q

Rock, D. (2009) *Your brain at work: Strategies for overcoming distraction, regaining focus, and working smarter all day long*. New York: HarperBusiness.

Rohn, J. (2003). *The art of exceptional living* [Audio]. New York: Simon & Schuster.

Sedlmeier, P., Eberth, J., Schwarz, M., Zimmermann, D., Haarig, F., Jaeger, S., et al. (2012). The psychological effects of meditation: A meta-analysis. *Psychological Bulletin, 138*(6), 1139–1171.

Seligman, M. E. P. (2013). *Flourish: A visionary new understanding of happiness and well-being*. New York: Free Press.

Sirota, M. (2010). Understanding messiness and hoarding [blog post]. *Dr. Marcia Sirota, M.D.* Retrieved from http://marciasirotamd.com/truth-about-addiction/understanding-messiness-and-hoarding-by-marcia-sirota

Strauss, C., Taylor, B. L., Gu, J., Kuyken, W., Baer, R., Jones, F., et al. (2016). What is compassion and how can we measure it? A review of definitions and measures. *Clinical Psychology Review, 47*, 15–27.

Tang, Y. Y., Holzel, B. K., & Posner, M. I. (2015). The neuroscience of mindfulness meditation. *Nature Reviews Neuroscience, 16*(4), 213–225.

Tierney, J. (2011, August 17). Do you suffer from decision fatigue? *New York Times Magazine*. Retrieved from www.nytimes.com/2011/08/21/magazine/do-you-suffer-from-decision-fatigue.html

Tracy, B. (2007). *Eat that frog: 21 great ways to stop procrastinating and get more done in less time*. Oakland, CA: Berrett-Koehler.

University of Washington. (2014). Healthy vs. unhealthy relationships. *Hall Health Center*. Retrieved from http://depts.washington.edu/hhpccweb/health-resource/healthy-vs-unhealthy-relationships

Warren, R. (2002). *The purpose-driven life: What on earth am I here for?* Grand Rapids, MI: Zondervan.

Weisinger, H. (2015). *Performing under pressure: The science of doing your best when it matters most*. New York: Crown Business.

Whitaker, T. (2012). *Shifting the monkey: The art of protecting good people from liars, criers, and other slackers*. Bloomington, IN: Solution Tree.

Index

The letter *f* following a page number denotes a figure.

About the Author

 **PJ Caposey** is an award-winning educator and author of six books. PJ served as the Oregon High School principal for four years and is currently serving in his fifth year as the superintendent of Meridian 223. Both districts experienced incredible turnarounds and received multiple national recognitions under PJ's leadership. PJ is also a sought-after keynote presenter, consultant, and professional development provider and has spoken at many local, state, and national conferences specializing in school culture, continuous improvement, social media, and teacher evaluation.

WHOLE CHILD
TENETS

The ASCD Whole Child approach is an effort to transition from a focus on narrowly defined academic achievement to one that promotes the long-term development and success of all children. Through this approach, ASCD supports educators, families, community members, and policymakers as they move from a vision about educating the whole child to sustainable, collaborative actions.

Manage Your Time or Time Will Manage You relates to the **supported** tenet.

For more about the ASCD Whole Child approach, visit **www.ascd.org/wholechild**.

1 **HEALTHY**
Each student enters school healthy and learns about and practices a healthy lifestyle.

2 **SAFE**
Each student learns in an environment that is physically and emotionally safe for students and adults.

3 **ENGAGED**
Each student is actively engaged in learning and is connected to the school and broader community.

4 **SUPPORTED**
Each student has access to personalized learning and is supported by qualified, caring adults.

5 **CHALLENGED**
Each student is challenged academically and prepared for success in college or further study and for employment and participation in a global environment.